Tony
BENNETT

Tony BENNETT

MATTHEW HOFFMAN

MetroBooks

MetroBooks

An Imprint of Friedman/Fairfax Publishers

Library of Congress Cataloging-in-Publication Data

Hoffman, Matthew.
    Tony Bennett: the best is yet to come / Matthew Hoffman.
        p.   cm.
    Includes bibliographical references and index.
    Discography: p.
    ISBN   1-56799-426-1   (hardcover)
    1.   Bennett, Tony, 1926-   2.   Singers—United States—Biography.
I. Title.
ML420.B3438H64   1997
782.42164'092—dc21
    [B]   96-50281

Editor: Stephen Slaybaugh
Art Director: Lynne Yeamans
Designer: Andrea Karman
Photography Editors: Wendy Missan and Dorian Romer

Color separations by Ocean Graphic International Company Ltd.
Printed in China by Leefung-Asco Printers Ltd.

1 3 5 7 9 10 8 6 4 2

For bulk purchases and special sales, please contact:
Friedman∕Fairfax Publishers
Attention: Sales Department
15 West 26th Street
New York, NY 10010
212∕685-6610 FAX 212∕685-1307

Visit our website:
http://www.metrobooks.com

ACKNOWLEDGMENTS

I would like to thank the following individuals and organizations, without whom this book
would have been impossible:

Elisha and Charles Abrams, Robin Brownstein, Robert, Barbara, Bryant Cooper at the Musuem of
Television and Radio, Drew and David Hoffman, J. David and Lora Hoffman, Peter Guttmacher,
Janette Jensen, Chuck Niles, Marilyn Saunders, Dan Singer, Stephen Slaybaugh, Elizabeth Viscott
Sullivan, Rachael, Wesley and Tess Wei, Richard Weisman, Blair Whittington, Gerald Zeigerman, The
Beverly Hills Library, The Brand Music Library, The Margaret Herrick Library, Eliott Hoffman,
and of course, Tony Bennett.

CONT

ENTS

Chapter One

ONCE UPON A TIME

The consummate performer, Tony Bennett
beams in response to the applause of his
appreciative fans.

In 1926, two events occurred that would forever change the face of American popular music. At the Warner Theater in New York, *Don Juan* introduced the public to talking motion pictures. In the same city, three days earlier, Anthony Dominick Benedetto was born. While the Vitaphone Company's advance in motion picture sound paved the way for lavish Hollywood musicals and, ultimately, music videos, the young Benedetto would go on to become one of the greatest popular singers of the twentieth century—Tony Bennett.

Born August 3, 1926, to Anna and John Benedetto, little Anthony grew up in Astoria, a neighborhood in the borough of Queens, New York City, with his elder brother and sister. John Benedetto, a tailor, had immigrated from the Calabria region of Italy around 1922. Shortly after settling in Manhattan, Benedetto met and married Anna Surace, who had been born in Little Italy in Manhattan near Mott and Hester Streets. Before Tony was born, his father had opened his first grocery store at Sixth Avenue and Fifty-second

Street in Manhattan—an ideal location in the heart of the city. Years later, the building in which the grocery was situated would become the CBS Building, home of Columbia Records (a label for which Bennett would record nearly one

hundred albums). Around the time that his younger son was born, Benedetto, plagued with poor health, took the advice of a doctor and moved from the city to the more sedate neighborhood of Astoria.

Queens, which boasts the largest area of New York's five boroughs, developed mostly during the 1940s. When the Benedetto family relocated to Astoria in the mid-1920s, the area was much more bucolic than it is today. Bennett remembers it as "farm country," complete with sheep and goats, rather than part of a teeming metropolis.

Astoria was initially a German and then an Italian neighborhood. In recent years, the influx of immigrants to this Queens neighborhood has been predominantly from Greece, earning Astoria the nickname "Little Greece." It has been said that more Greeks can be found in Astoria than anyplace in the world—except Athens.

When Bennett reflects on those early days, he describes life in the Benedetto household as a joyous affair, where everybody "felt good about life," striving to get through the work week. "Every weekend, all the uncles on my

A young Tony posed for this photo in the 1930s. He already had a sense of style.

Years before singing about his "city by the bay," the singer posed for pictures in his city by the Hudson.

mother's side of the family would come over with all the nieces and nephews, and we would take out mandolins and guitars and entertain each other. My older brother and sister and I couldn't wait to entertain the relatives. It was the Depression. Everybody needed everybody else."

At these gatherings, the three Benedetto siblings stood at the center of the family circle. John Jr. sang, Mary presided as mistress of ceremonies, and Tony provided counterbalance by clowning around, doing impersonations of Al Jolson, Bing Crosby, and Eddie Cantor. Lack of material wealth and economic stability brought this Italian-American family together to share those resources they had in abundance—love and strength. "I remember the good vibrations, the warm feeling that we got from one another, and the fun we had."

Musical talent was the other asset generously distributed among the family. Bennett's natural musical talent was likely furthered by the influence of his relatives in his formative years. One of the anecdotes related in the Benedetto family was that of John Benedetto singing from a mountaintop in Italy with his voice carrying throughout the valley below. On American soil, John Benedetto had only

IT'S IN THE GENES

When interviewed by Linda Brandi Catuera for her book Growing Up Italian, *Bennett declared that "Italians have it in their genes to excel in music and art" and "It's a known fact that Italian-Americans have made good pop singers." Although genetic scientists would be hard-pressed to isolate the precise gene to which Bennett refers, there appears to be ample empirical data to support his hypothesis. Bennett bolsters his theory with compelling evidence: Vic Damone, Perry Como, Dean Martin, and "the king of the entertainment world," Frank Sinatra. Quod erat demonstrandum.*

to reach an audience of one, as he often sang to his younger son.

While Bennett may have inherited his voice from his father, it was his elder brother, John, who provided him with the spur to make something of that inheritance. Although Antonio first hit the boards in school plays, operettas, and Queens minstrel shows when he was seven years old, John Benedetto was singing with the children's chorus at the Metropolitan Opera at the age of fourteen. The excited Benedetto clan, thrilled to have one of its own pursuing the great Italian tradition, referred to him as "The Little Caruso," and declared, "Oh, we have an opera singer." Bennett recalls having been quite envious, but this sibling rivalry was not about bitterness. Instead, it brought out a competitive spirit and gentle one-upmanship that would serve Bennett well for the years to come. "I started showing off, and have been doing it ever since," Bennett says.

LOSS AND RECOVERY

When Bennett was nine years old, tragedy struck. His father went into the hospital with appendicitis and never returned home. The so-called miracle sulfa drugs were not yet available, and John Benedetto died of infection. To

OPPOSITE: Outside his home, Bennett converses with the neighborhood children. The rake appears to be brand new and, as of yet, unused. **ABOVE:** A youthful Bennett, looking somewhat bemused, poses for the camera.

A portrait of the artist as a young man, captured in a more casual sartorial moment.

Good Material: "Work with the Best"

Bennett has been asked to compromise his artistic integrity a number of times throughout his career. Initially, with the onslaught of rock 'n' roll in the mid-1950s, Bennett was pressured to sing rock. In the late 1960s, Bennett was again urged to record the hits of the day. In neither case would Bennett give in to record-company demands that he record only material with strictly commercial appeal. Looking back, Bennett acknowledges that his creative integrity came from his mother: "As a seamstress, she never worked on a cheap or badly conceived dress. The only time I ever saw her get angry was the day she had a bad dress to work on. Later on, I found myself subconsciously turning down all bad songs and realizing only much later that I learned about refusing the second-rate from her. If I am going to do a song, I want to sing the very best song and not compromise. That is what she taught us: work with the best. Not to compromise is a marvelous thing to learn."

this day, Bennett cannot think back to that time without getting a lump in his throat.

Anna Benedetto worked at home as a seamstress for the garment industry to support her family. In order to reduce the strain of making a living, raising a family, and dealing with her grief, she sent her youngest to live with an uncle for six months; John and Mary stayed home. When Bennett discovered that he alone was sent away, it hurt him deeply. Having lost his father, he was now further traumatized by separation from what was left of the family unit, and his resentment lasted for years. However, the pain and anger would be tempered, for this period prepared Bennett psychologically and emotionally for years on the road. "Things really work out for the best. Because that experience taught me how to adjust to being alone. Now I actually like it. On the road, I don't feel I'm missing something by not being rooted....It taught me to be alone and be satisfied with it. You need that if you're an artist."

Bennett's artistry was nurtured at the High School of Industrial Art in Manhattan, where he studied music and painting, but his decision to become a singer must be traced back to a hot summer Sunday—July 11, 1936, when the Triborough Bridge complex was to be dedicated at noon and a parade from Queens converged with a parade from Manhattan. Bennett marched at the front of the Queens contingent, attired in a white silk suit. "My mother put me next to Mayor LaGuardia. I was the little mascot of the parade from Queens. We all sang 'Marching Along Together,' and everybody was so happy and cheerful. Every time I turned around, I

Anna Benedetto and her famous son on the town. Bennett's mother instilled a sense of strength and integrity that served the artist well through years of struggle.

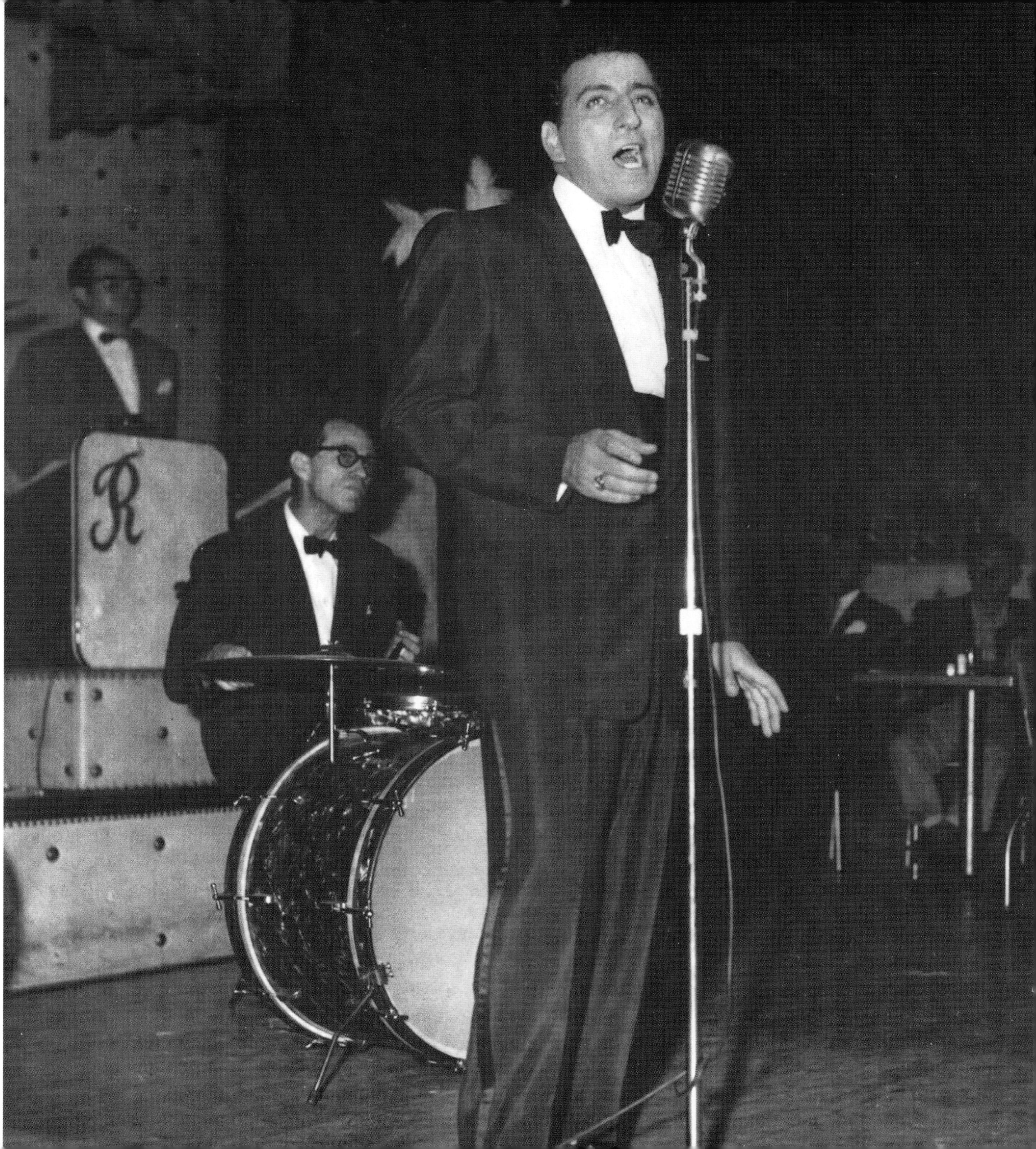

FIORELLO LaGUARDIA

Mayor Fiorello LaGuardia, at his desk—a great man managing the affairs of a great city.

It is appropriate that the experience that Bennett regards as the wellspring for his career involves Mayor Fiorello LaGuardia. Nicknamed "The Little Flower," LaGuardia, elected in 1934, put an end to the corruption that ran rampant in New York City politics. LaGuardia managed to maintain a positive outlook for a city swamped by a $30 million debt at the height of the Great Depression. Indeed, by the end of his tenure in 1945, LaGuardia had reduced crime, introduced vast social reform, and restored economic stability. Like LaGuardia, Tony Bennett is a man of ideals.

saw somebody smiling from ear to ear. When I entertain, I am trying to make people feel good, and I know it all came from that day. Everybody was so positive. It was a special kind of day."

Bennett's first professional job, for which he earned $15, was at the age of thirteen, singing at a Democratic club beer party in Astoria. Throughout his early teens, Bennett would sing on his own in any of the small clubs that would allow him. On weekends, Bennett made an effort to supplement the family income as a singing waiter at Ricardo's in Astoria Park. Bennett's talent, as yet undeveloped, did not win many fans, and his friends often made matters worse by attending these performances only to shout and

throw peanuts at the young singer. None of this seemed to faze Bennett, who continued to work as a teen performer despite less-than-appreciative audiences.

In general, Bennett's schoolmates did not take his artistic endeavors seriously. As a youth, Bennett rendered enormous, beautiful chalk murals on the streets of Astoria. A source of awe and wonder to mothers and children, these works were treated with little respect by Bennett's contemporaries, who would play football over the drawings.

Fortunately, Bennett's teachers were much more encouraging. Bennett showed great skill and aptitude as a graphic artist and seemed to be on the path to a career as a commercial artist. Curiously, it was at the High School of

OPPOSITE: A 1951 promotional handout of the up-and-coming singer. In the more intimate club setting, the separation between the stage and the audience is negligible. **ABOVE:** Benedetto, the artist, puts brush to canvas for one of his many famous landscape paintings.

Industrial Art that an instructor told Bennett, "You have to go into the music business." Another teacher, upon encountering the young chalk muralist, gave words of praise and invited Bennett to paint watercolors with him in the park. This recognition and the subsequent watercolor session was so pleasant that it imparted Bennett with a lifelong avocation: "To this day, I'm still painting and watercoloring."

THE WORLD AT WAR

Shortly after his graduation from high school, Bennett was drafted and began a brief military stint during the final days of World War II. During this period, Bennett would perform for his fellow Special Services Unit troops. It was also at this time, when confronted with the horrors of the war, that Bennett developed the social conscience and humanistic ideology for which he has long been known. It would have been very easy for an American of Bennett's generation to get caught up in the jingoism of the era, but he "couldn't avoid see-

ing the ridiculous incongruities." For example, when Bennett's infantry arrived in the German city of Mannheim. The bombings had leveled virtually all the humble dwellings but left the massive Ford plant standing.

Absurd contradictions extended from the frontline to the American officers' mess. Bennett's invitation to Frank Smith, a high school friend and a black soldier, to join him for Thanksgiving dinner provoked a southern lieutenant's ire. The lieutenant, who was presumably fighting to liberate oppressed Europe, rebuked Bennett for bringing a black person into the dining room and commanded the two soldiers to repair to the kitchen. Bennett refused to follow orders and angrily stormed out with his friend. This act of insubordination cost Bennett his corporal stripes. Consequently, Bennett was demoted to private and assigned the wretched duty of exhuming mass graves and identifying soldiers' bodies.

All of Bennett's wartime associations did not have such dire consequences. In fact, toward the end of his military service, Bennett was able to visit various army bases and give jazz concerts. The pianist with whom he toured was Fred Katz, who was to be a pivotal contact for Bennett in the entertainment industry.

ABOVE: In the early days before he hit the big time, Bennett sang in a neighborhood spot. The patrons of the establishment seem to be unaware that they are in the presence of greatness. PAGE 22: Before a big band, with a swinging horn section, Bennett belted one out to the back of the house. PAGE 23: On his way to Chicago from New York City, in the summer of 1961, Bennett paused to photograph his TWA hostess.

TRAINING UNDER THE GI BILL

Stateside, Bennett was able to take advantage of the GI Bill, which allowed veterans to choose their own place of study or job training. Bennett enrolled at the American Theater Wing's Professional School and studied voice and bel canto with Miriam Spier and Peter D'Andrea. Spier instructed, "Don't imitate singers. Instead, be influenced by musicians and how they phrase, so you won't sound like anybody but yourself."

Bennett was in good hands. After all, Spier was responsible for coaching female singing stars Helen O'Connell and Peggy Lee. But despite excellent mentors and diligently applying himself to his craft, Bennett did not pass any auditions. For income, he held a variety of jobs: elevator operator at the Park Sheraton hotel, grocery store clerk, runner for the Associated Press, and singing waiter.

It was at the Shangri-La, a small club in Astoria, that Bennett had his first taste of real professionalism. Tyree Glenn, a

MIRIAM SPIER AND ALEC WILDER

Nearly twenty years after studying with Miriam Spier, Bennett was still nostalgic and sentimental about those early days. When Columbia Records renewed his contract in 1968, Bennett requested that Columbia president Clive Davis and he commemorate the event by being photographed not in the CBS Building, but across the street in front of the brownstone where he had studied with Miriam Spier.

Bennett first met composer and lyricist Alec Wilder at Spier's brownstone. Two decades later, Wilder commented, "He believes. I know that he has never ceased to respect quality in a writer, both lyrically and musically; and to insist throughout his career on singing the good song—as opposed to the topical song or the immediate song, or the song that would make him more money. He challenges fashion. He takes chances—and he wins. And how nice for people like me! His belief is based on his enormous need to communicate. You can feel the need when you hear him sing a tune. You know that this is a lot more than 'being a public figure.' He sings to the individual, not to a public or an audience. Furthermore, he is the only star I've ever met who opens his own door!"

trombonist, overheard Bennett singing and invited him onstage to sing with his group. For a struggling artist, a little reassurance can go a long way. This kindness, which Bennett would never forget, encouraged him to persevere in his pursuit of a singing career.

The 1940s were coming to an end, and the chances of success seemed distant to the struggling Bennett. It was all the would-be crooner could do to make ends meet. When Bennett considers those days of scuffling, he comments, "It never mattered to me as long as I was singing. I promised myself I would always sing wherever I landed—at the top or at the bottom. If I had to be a singing waiter tomorrow, I'd grab it. I just love standing there, belting it out."

At the turn of the decade, Bennett unexpectedly found himself on a springboard that gave his career a considerable boost. Seemingly overnight, Bennett was launched to a position where he could share his love of singing with quite a few more people than a handful of denizens at an Astoria eatery.

RAGS
TO
RICHES

"TONY IS ABSOLUTELY TERRIFIC." —BOB HOPE

In 1950, television was still in its infancy. There were only 1.5 million television sets in the United States (a year later, there would be approximately ten times as many). It was through this nascent medium that Bennett was first exposed to the greater American public. The show was *Arthur Godfrey's Talent Scouts*, a pleasant vehicle that sought to introduce young unknown performers through a weekly competition. Although the first prize the week Bennett was on the show ultimately went to future singing star Rosemary Clooney, Tony placed second.

Watching was Jan Murray, who had a television show of his own, *Songs for Sale*, which showcased the compositions of amateur songwriters. Murray was impressed with Clooney and Bennett and invited them both to appear on his show. Nothing was to come directly from either of these appearances, but Bennett's outlook was much improved. Shortly after this brief foray into television, Bennett returned to a more familiar, intimate medium—the nightclub.

Pearl Bailey, an entertainer so beloved by her public that she became known as "Aunt Pearl," was conducting auditions at the Greenwich Village Inn for what was supposed to be an all-black revue. Enter Bennett, who at the time was performing under the moniker Joe Bari. (Bari is the port city in Italy where Bennett's father was raised.) Bailey was instantly taken with Bennett's talent and hired him on as a production singer. This position required Bennett to split his duties between

singing and acting as master of ceremonies. Bailey's belief in Bennett was so strong that when the owner of the nightclub appeared unwilling to employ Bennett, she countered with a threat: "Either this boy stays on my show, or I'm not playing here."

The magnanimous Bailey, who had a sharp eye for talent, could foresee Bennett's destiny. Concerned about the dangers of too much too fast, Aunt Pearl proffered the following advice to her young charge: "You're going to have a lot of success, but don't let that helium hit your brain and make you fly away from us. Keep your feet on the ground." Bailey projected, "It takes ten years to learn what to do and not to do on stage. You can look awful good at the beginning, but that doesn't mean you can sustain." Bennett must have been doing something right, for Bailey could never have predicted the speed with which success was to arrive.

HOPE SPRINGS ETERNAL

During the engagement of Bailey's revue, a special guest, also in the entertainment business, was sitting in the audience one night— Bob Hope. Hope was in town with Jane Russell, in a variety show at the Paramount Theater. Taking a break from a hectic schedule of four shows a day, Hope came to see headliner Bailey but was so enchanted by Bennett that he invited him to appear onstage with him the next evening.

It was the closing night of the Paramount show, and before introducing his new discovery to the audience, Hope concerned himself with one small detail. Hope thought that "Joe Bari" was not a good stage name and inquired after the singer's real name. "Anthony Benedetto" did

ABOVE: Bob Hope— after years of "Road" pictures with Bing Crosby—helped to make Tony Bennett a household name after only ten days on the road with the singer. PAGES 28–29: Sheet music in hand, Bennett takes a well-deserved break and relaxes between takes in the studio.

BOB HOPE AT THE PARAMOUNT

not look any more marquee-friendly. Hope pondered an alias for the unknown balladeer and then, without consulting the nervous Benedetto, announced, "And here's a new singer, Tony Bennett!" The introduction had to be repeated; the newly christened troubadour did not know whom Hope was talking about! Bennett sang just two songs and brought down the house. Hope bounded onstage, seized the microphone, and motioning for silence, adressed the crowd: "He doesn't know it yet, but I'm taking him along for a tour of the United States. He also doesn't know it, but from now on his name is going to be Tony Bennett."

Hope was true to his word. The next day, Bennett joined ranks with the likes of Les Brown and Marilyn Maxwell for a ten-day tour of the United States. During this tour, Hope, the seasoned professional, offered Bennett a crash course in the art of navigating the stage. Bennett recalls, "He actually showed me what to do on the stage and how to perform. He told me, 'Come out smiling. Show

Bob Hope, an English-born American entertainer, knew a thing or two about good stage names. Before dubbing Tony Bennett, Hope had to deal with his own nom de théâtre. Before settling on a show-business career, Hope boxed under the name "Packy East." Performing under his given name, Leslie Townes Hope, the performer found himself nearly unemployable on the Windy City's vaudeville circut of 1928. When it dawned on him that the androgynous name Leslie might have been too ambiguous for the citizens of Al Capone's Chicago, Hope changed his first name to Bob. Under his new, more masculine name, Hope went from $10 a show to $25 and, very soon after, $250 per week—big money in those days.

Hope is responsible for decades of overseas Christmas tours for American troops stationed in combat zones. When Bennett was solicited by Hope for one such tour, he responded that it was against his religion: "I'm a devout coward."

The Paramount Theater figures heavily in the evolution of Tony Bennett. In addition to being the arena in which Bennett was introduced to the world under his permanent stage name, the Paramount served as classroom. "I got my musical education by playing hooky and listening to Sinatra at the Paramount. He opened up a whole new bag with the microphone, the artful use of intimate singing to show psychology, real thinking."

the people you like them.' To this day, I still follow those rules."

OUT OF THE CLUBS AND INTO THE STUDIO

In addition to playing small clubs and cabarets, Bennett had the good luck to learn his craft during the final days of vaudeville. As a child, Bennett would listen with rapt attention as his uncle, an ex-vaudeville hoofer, related stories of actors and singers perfecting their acts as they traveled back and forth across the country. Fortunately, there was still enough of a circuit on which the unseasoned artist could refine his act. Bennett recollects, "It was a great school, because you were allowed to go from one town to another to get rid of your mistakes, to take a song and hone it to perfection."

In 1949, Marty Manning, a musical arranger readying floor-show acts, introduced Bennett to Tony Tamburello, who was engaged to put

"If Tony Bennett, who swing sings wonderfully, can't send you, there's a psychiatrist right up the street from you. Dig him." —Louis Armstrong

"Because" of You"

When Bennett recorded "Because of You," the song had been gathering dust for more than a decade. The authors, Dudley Wilkinson and Arthur Hammerstein (uncle of Oscar Hammerstein II, librettist and lyricist of Oklahoma! *and* South Pacific), *had given up on the song, which had never caught on. When the song hit, eighty-two-year-old Hammerstein remarked that it made him feel "thirty years younger." The royalties must have helped.*

routines together for the shows. One of the routines began with "Boulevard of Broken Dreams," an old Russ Columbo tune.

Russ Columbo, a singer and songwriter, enjoyed popularity in the early 1930s on radio and went on to star in the movies. He had made only three feature films when a tragic accident ended his career. A match struck against an ancient dueling pistol, which he used as a paperweight, caused the supposedly unloaded weapon to discharge. Columbo was killed when the ricochet hit him in the head.

Bennett would have better luck with the tune than did the hapless Columbo. "Boulevard of Broken Dreams" was one of the two songs Bennett chose to sing at his debut at the Paramount Theater. By April 1950, Bennett had breathed new life into the song, which became a vehicle ideally suited to show off his voice.

Word spread to Mitch Miller, the head of the Popular Artists and Repertoire department at Columbia Records, that there was a new kid in

town, and boy, could he sing. Miller contacted Bennett's manager at the time, Raymond G. Muscarella, a Brooklyn businessman who was instrumental in developing Vic Damone's career. Muscarella submitted a demonstration record on which Tamburello provided piano accompaniment. Miller, pleased with the product, offered Bennett an exclusive recording contract. "Boulevard of Broken Dreams" was rerecorded and released as a single.

When Bennett reassesses the record, he admits, "The first recording was just saying, 'Look how good I sing.'" It is true that Bennett attacks "Boulevard of Broken Dreams" con brio and with an abundance of vibrato, but the sheer exuberance of the recording prompts the listener to forgive those excesses.

Half a million record buyers found it in their hearts to pardon Bennett's youthful indulgence. On the basis of the widespread popularity of that single disc, Bennett was invited to perform at clubs across the United States.

Enjoying the good life, Bennett looks positively ecstatic leaning on the hood of his new set of wheels.

LOOKING FOR A HIT

The road to fame is bumpy at best, and the lane change from "Boulevard of Broken Dreams" to "Easy Street" was a difficult maneuver. Although Bennett scored a moderate success with his first record, Miller and conductor Percy Faith were getting antsy. Artistry aside, the record industry is a business, and in the absence of a follow-up hit, Bennett was about to be dropped from the Columbia label at the beginning of 1951. He needed a hit record—and fast.

In the effort to produce a hit, Bennett attempted everything "from being a race singer to trying to do a Mario Lanza." Ultimately, they settled on a Percy Faith arrangement with strings, in which Bennett would "just sing sincerely and honestly." This was the ticket. As a final track, in a session that lasted less than four hours, Bennett recorded "Because of You." The song was recorded in the first week of April 1951. By the end of June, "Because of You" hit the

MITCH MILLER, A.K.A. "THE BEARD"

History has been unkind to Mitch Miller and Percy Faith. If not entirely forgotten, they are too easily dismissed as merely part of the machinery at Columbia Records. Faith's masterful arrangements and Miller's exquisite production and extensive coaching allowed for the ascendancy of Bennett, Rosemary Clooney, Johnny Mathis, Frankie Laine, and many other singing stars.

From 1961 to 1965, Miller hosted and conducted the orchestra of the television show Sing Along with Mitch *on NBC. The musical hour, which featured a male chorus of twenty-five and regular female solo vocalists, grew out of Miller's popular* Sing Along *albums. Although Miller's name is primarily associated with this light entertainment, it would be a mistake to overlook his musical genius.*

When jazz legend Charlie Parker wanted to record with strings, Miller, then at Mercury Records, was selected by the president of Verve Records, Norman Granz, to do the A&R work. (Miller also played oboe on the sessions.) The result, a glorious marriage of bebop and orchestral music, fulfilled one of Parker's dreams — the hit album Charlie Parker with Strings. *Miller earned the nickname "The Beard" for wearing a beard at a time when it was not the fashion.*

charts, where it remained for thirty-two weeks, ten of them in the number one position.

In late July, "Cold, Cold Heart" was released while "Because of You" remained at the top of the charts. "Cold, Cold Heart," a Hank Williams composition, was a musical oddity in that it was essentially a folksy country song given the Percy Faith string treatment. Despite its peculiar hybrid nature, "Cold, Cold Heart" shot up the charts and peaked at number one, where it stayed for six weeks.

Two hits in the top ten had a dramatic effect on Bennett's fame and fortune. By autumn of 1951, Bennett's salary for his singing engagements had taken a quantum leap. Five years earlier, Bennett was making $15 a week at the Pheasant Tavern in Astoria. Now he was pulling in $3,500 a week at the Paramount Theater. The adulation of swooning bobby-soxers for Bennett was reminiscent of that shown for Sinatra in the early 1940s. At the end of 1951, *Cashbox* magazine named Bennett male vocalist of the year.

At a recording session in New York, Columbia Records' master producer Mitch Miller goes over the charts with Bennett.

GET OUT YOUR HANDKERCHIEFS

Back in New York, Bennett was mobbed by two thousand female fans during personal appearances in Brooklyn. At his opening at the Paramount, Bennett mixed publicity stunt with fan appreciation when he personally presented red roses to the first five hundred women.

It is an all-too-familiar image: a mob of adoring fans descends upon the popular singer and tears at his clothing in search of souvenirs. During these close encounters, Bennett noticed that his breast-pocket handkerchief was being filched regularly by eager memento seekers. Rather than defend himself against future assaults, Bennett jovially cooperated—his handkerchiefs bore the message "Borrowed from Tony Bennett."

When Bennett returned to the Paramount Theater at the beginning of 1952, his salary had been raised to an astounding $4,000 a week. *Time* magazine referred to Bennett as the "Idol of the Girls." Indeed, Bennett's audience was largely made up of a throng of squealing

The Paramount Theater, 1953. In less than three years, Bennett had come a long way—from his two-song debut as an unlisted act on Bob Hope's bill to a returning headliner.

girls. Bennett enjoyed the acclaim but felt that the hysteria surrounding the shows detracted from his true creative endeavor. In a subsequent interview with *Time*, Bennett protested, "This isn't the kind of singing I want to do. I can go out on stage and crush them every time—they'd stand on their hands for me. But I don't like being sensational that way. If I could sing the way I like to sing—naturally— I'd be a better entertainer. It'll take from six months to a year to get the right arrangements and the right songs, but that's what I'm going to do."

At twenty-five years old, Bennett had declared what was to be the manifesto for his entire performing career. From this point on, Bennett used live performance to woodshed new tunes before he put them on wax. "I live with these songs. I study them. I work them for six months sometimes. With the reality of an audience reaction, it's surprising how your interpretation changes."

There were other changes. His finances much improved. Bennett was able to buy his mother a house in River Edge, New Jersey, where she could retire. And on February 12, 1952, two thousand girls wearing black veils mourned outside New York City's Saint Patrick's Cathedral when Bennett married Patricia Beech, a fan he had met in Cleveland.

During a welcome break from his busy performance schedule of 1953, Bennett shows his sketches to his wife, Patricia.

Back at Columbia Records, Bennett continued to produce hit records. "Blue Velvet" charted in the top twenty, and "Rags to Riches," a song whose title seemed to refer to Bennett's success, marked a third number one hit for the singing star. Curiously enough, Bennett had little desire to record the tune and was practically forced to do so by Miller and Faith. "Rags to Riches" remained on the charts for nearly half the year.

Numerous artists had recorded "Stranger in Paradise," a song from the Broadway musical *Kismet* but Bennett's recording with the Ray Charles Singers climbed to the top ten, stopping just shy of the summit, at the number-two position. This string of hits improved Bennett's standing at Columbia and provided the leverage needed to campaign for his pet project—an album. This was a radical concept. In those days, popular artists recorded singles, not albums. Nonetheless, Bennett pleaded his case for months and was finally permitted to record a

Two years before Bennett was born, the "acoustic" age of sound recording was replaced by the electrical process. The new era offered greater realism and better sound reproduction. Two years before Bennett entered the recording studio, Columbia Records introduced the long-playing (LP) record, which offered improved sound quality and longer playing time. Fortunately, Bennett's original masters have been well preserved. Most of the songs mentioned in this book can be found on Forty Years: The Artistry of Tony Bennett, *a four-disc set compiled by Sony Music Entertainment, Inc. for Columbia Records.*

The more ardent collector of Bennett memorabilia would do best to visit curio shops or contact rare-record collecting services in order to locate the original albums from which the tunes were selected for Forty Years. *Bennett's recorded output is so voluminous as to preclude rerelease of the entire catalog in the compact-disc format.*

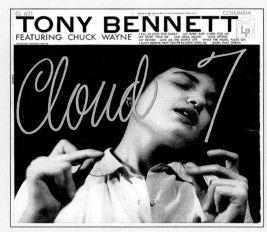

The cover of Bennett's pet project, <u>Cloud 7</u>. Judging from the photograph of the female in finger-snapping, eyes-closed ecstasy, perhaps the album should have been entitled <u>Cloud 9</u>.

collection of tunes released under the title *Cloud 7*.

On *Cloud 7*, Bennett fulfilled a long-held desire to record "While the Music Plays On." Sung in the first person by a Pagliaccio like character, "While the Music Plays On" relates a tale in which the singer serenades, through tears, his loved one as she passes by in the arms of another. Bennett had been perfecting this song long before signing on with Columbia, and the hard work is evident. The vocal pyrotechnics of his first records have been replaced with a greater maturity and refinement. Bennett delivers an exquisitely subtle, heart-wrenching performance, and sideman Charles Panely lends a gorgeous trumpet solo to the composition.

Cloud 7 is also significant in that Bennett temporarily departed from his winning formula at Columbia by enlisting guitarist Chuck Wayne to arrange and conduct. Clearly, Bennett was growing more secure with his talent and wanted to stretch.

Bennett and Rock 'n' Roll

The Generation Gap

In the early winter months of 1956, the popular music world experienced a seismic disturbance that would drastically shift demographics and forever alter the way recording artists were marketed. Newly signed RCA recording artist Elvis Presley hit the charts with "Heartbreak Hotel." Rock 'n' roll was here to stay, but surely there was room for Bennett and others performing standards—so one would have thought.

Suddenly, a great divide split American popular culture. Teenagers, representing the heart of the record-buying public, swarmed to the new music, leaving Bennett and his colleagues in the dust. The same fans who but five years earlier exhibited advanced cases of Bennettmania were now converts to a new sound calculated to capture their hearts and pocketbooks.

On a return visit to the Paramount Theater, Bennett found himself being booed off the stage just a few bars into

There was a lot of money to be had for the artist willing to jump on the rock 'n' roll bandwagon. Bennett resisted. "I knew a lot of those guys would clean up. I still couldn't sing any of that stuff," claims Bennett. It is probable that Bennett would have lost the core of his loyal audience, those who "liked to hear the good things, songs with lyrics that told a story," had he compromised. Ralph Sharon, Bennett's longtime accompanist and arranger, avers, "If Tony had embraced rock 'n' roll, his career would have fizzled, because he had no feeling for it."

Bennett (who once referred to Elvis Presley as "the first Coca-Cola bottle that was a human being. He was made into a commodity") has his own theory as to the father of rock 'n' roll. Bennett cites Johnny Ray as the performer who turned the music scene around. (Perhaps a debt of loyalty to his first producer resides in this assessment. Ray's hit "Cry," produced by Mitch Miller, sold 2 million copies.) Bennett asserts that the turning point was during an engagement at London's Palladium, when Ray, who was deaf, became anxious and lost himself in Jerry Lee Lewis–like abandon, tearing down curtains and banging on the piano. According to Bennett, the fans went wild, and Ray was sold out for six weeks.

"Stranger in Paradise." Looking back, Bennett cannot help but blame Alan Freed, producer of the ill-fated event, for much of the pervasive divisiveness that was to become part of the music industry. In an interview with Joseph Lanza in *Pulse*, Bennett remarked, "Alan Freed was the first one who said, 'This is your music, and your parents like the other kind of music.' That broke the families up."

The approach to winning an audience had changed considerably in less than a decade. Back when Bennett was playing seven shows a day at the Paramount, the management had instructed him to "sing songs that everybody liked. Not just the youth group. In the morning, we had the youth or teenagers. In the afternoon, we had the senior citizens. At night, we had the young lovers and married couples. By the end of the day, we had played the whole demographic: everybody."

Music promoters and record-company executives were much more interested in

turning a quick buck than in preserving some sacrosanct notion of family entertainment. Rock 'n' roll music created an opportunity for those in control of marketing to draw arbitrary boundaries and instigate generational conflict on a musical basis. The American public was divided and conquered.

The rock 'n' roll juggernaut stole a large segment of the youth audience, but Bennett maintained his popularity. Bennett's records were selling at a respectable rate, but the sales volume was well below what was needed to make the charts. In 1957, "Ça, C'est l'amour," a bouncy pop tune arranged by Neal Hefti, marked the last time a Bennett record would chart in the 1950s. "Ça, C'est l'amour" failed to make the top twenty, peaking at number twenty-two.

The charts have always been regarded by the music industry with the sort of awe due the Holy Grail. Three number-one hits undoubtedly gave Bennett's career the boost that made his name a household word, but Bennett looks

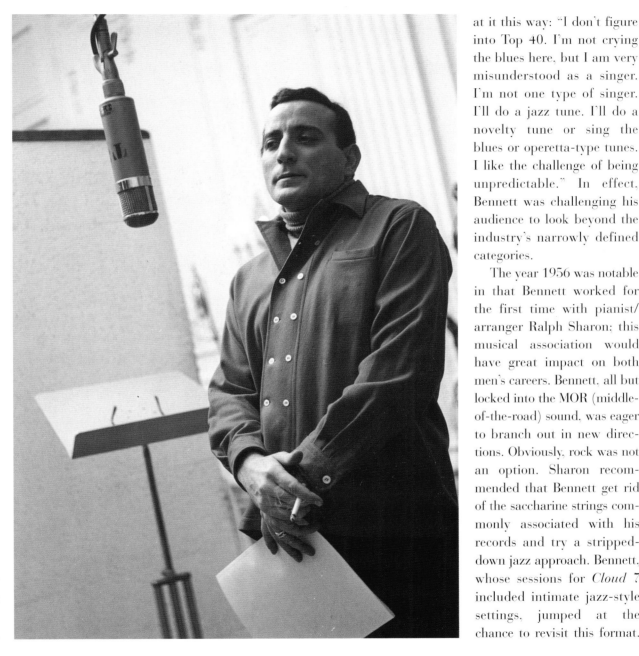

at it this way: "I don't figure into Top 40. I'm not crying the blues here, but I am very misunderstood as a singer. I'm not one type of singer. I'll do a jazz tune. I'll do a novelty tune or sing the blues or operetta-type tunes. I like the challenge of being unpredictable." In effect, Bennett was challenging his audience to look beyond the industry's narrowly defined categories.

The year 1956 was notable in that Bennett worked for the first time with pianist/arranger Ralph Sharon; this musical association would have great impact on both men's careers. Bennett, all but locked into the MOR (middle-of-the-road) sound, was eager to branch out in new directions. Obviously, rock was not an option. Sharon recommended that Bennett get rid of the saccharine strings commonly associated with his records and try a stripped-down jazz approach. Bennett, whose sessions for *Cloud 7* included intimate jazz-style settings, jumped at the chance to revisit this format.

OPPOSITE: In the Columbia Records studio, Bennett, in sartorial splendor, sings and swings. **ABOVE:** Beneath the boom mike, Bennett grabs a cigarette between takes.

BENNETT AND THE SMALL SCREEN

The result was *The Beat of My Heart*, a recording that employed notable jazz figures Art Blakey, Milt Hinton, Nat Adderly, Eddie Costa, Herbie Mann, and Chico Hamilton, to name but a few.

A highlight from this album, and one of Sharon's personal favorite songs in the collection, is "Lazy Afternoon." Bennett, accompanied by Sharon (piano), John Pisano (guitar), James Bond (bass), and Chico Hamilton (drums), paints a stunningly evocative portrait, rich in sensual imagery. Clearly, Bennett was not aiming to reclaim those fans who had defected to the rock camp. *The Beat of My Heart* did, however, win Bennett a new audience—jazz fans. Technically, Bennett has never been a jazz singer, but a pop singer, with jazz accoutrement—a style ultimately labeled "pop-jazz vocalist." Bennett points to this album as the watershed of his early career. In addition to expanding the base of his audience, it marked the beginning of an ongoing alliance with jazz music and jazz musicians.

Popular singer Perry Como on the set of his Saturday night television show, which Bennett would host as a summer replacement for two seasons.

Bennett was not overly impressed with the capacity of television to convey what he had to offer. In 1958, Bennett commented, "You can't build a bond between yourself and your audience on a little TV screen. The folks watching you in their living rooms may be in pajamas, stocking feet, or holding hands. You can't tell what kind of mood they're in or what they feel like seeing or hearing. I've always preferred to appear before live audiences, people I can see."

IN ONE ERA, OUT ANOTHER

Record sales lagging, Bennett continued to perform hundreds of concerts a year to full houses across North America. Bennett, at the top of his game as an entertainer, had developed an easy rapport with his audience. Crowd-pleasing show-stoppers like "Sing You Sinners" garnered Bennett an invitation to play Las Vegas. Meanwhile, Bennett's contract with Columbia Records required him to produce three albums a year.

In the summer of 1956, television beckoned when Perry Como asked Bennett to host his popular television show as a summer replacement for five weeks. Bennett accepted and was overcome with fear. Before this experience, Bennett had fought various bouts of stage fright; in the early days, overcome with doubt, Bennett would soak in a tub filled with ice cubes to calm his nerves before a daunting opening night. Frank Sinatra came to the res-

OPPOSITE: Upon his 1959 return to hosting Perry Presents, Bennett, clearly having overcome his stage fright, reveals an easy rapport with camera.

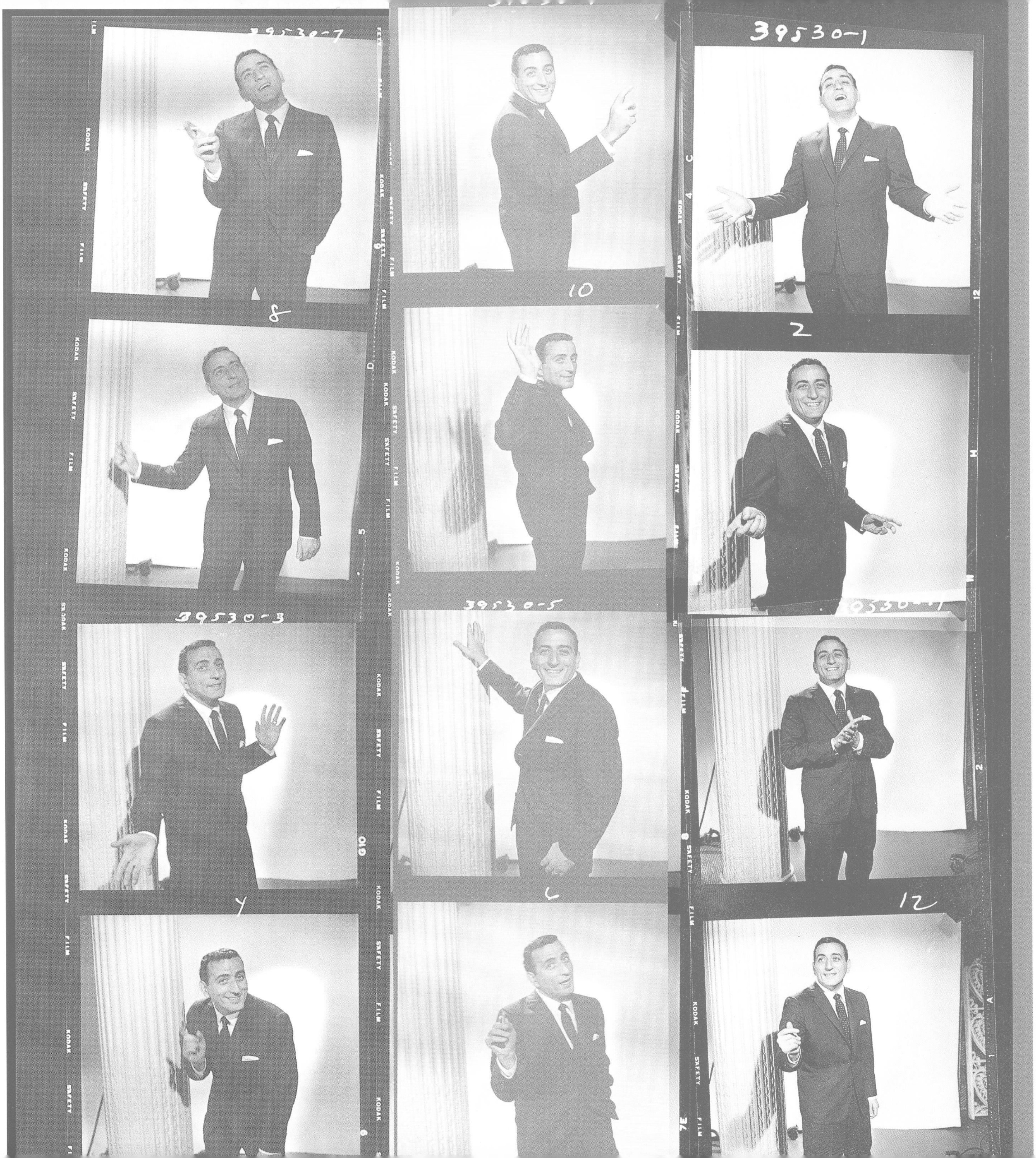
39530-1
39530-5
KODAK
SAFETY
FILM

cue and assured Bennett that "the public likes someone who's nervous, because then they know you're really concerned." Bennett relaxed and comported himself admirably. Como was impressed enough to invite Bennett back three seasons later to star on a thirteen-week series, *Perry Presents*.

This was to be Bennett's first long-run exposure on television. Bennett had been frustrated in the past when he was forced to bargain for extra time. "They never give you enough time to get your point across, to build an attitude with the audience." Bennett was finally getting a chance to show the vast American audience his act the way it should be seen. Bennett set out to re-create the effect of his stage act by playing to the studio audience, not to the camera. This approach had helped Bennett establish the correct

attitude during his appearances on *The Steve Allen Show*.

As the 1950s came to an end, Bennett was nowhere to be found on the charts. Appearances on television, on the radio, and in nightclubs generated enough interest to keep the sales of Bennett records in the black, but rock 'n' roll dominated the airwaves and accounted for a large portion of the records purchased. Since Bennett had become a mainstay of the Columbia Records catalog, there was no danger of his being dropped from the label, but surely Bennett, and especially Miller, would have welcomed some chart action. Life on the road was grueling and lonely. As much as Bennett enjoyed live performance, the accolades from night to night could not make up for the lack of a hit record. Bennett needed the vindication that attended a successful chart topper. Something had to give.

ABOVE: Bennett enjoys a visit with television host/musician/raconteur Steve Allen. OPPOSITE: When in Rome.... Bennett in shades for an engagement in Los Angeles at the famous outdoor amphitheater, the Hollywood Bowl, in 1961. PAGES 42–43: Bennett listens intently to jazz great Count Basie.

Chapter Three

I'LL BE AROUND

Bennett happily resigns himself to some assistance with his neckwear for a performance of "A Night at Minsky's" at the Dunes Hotel in Las Vegas.

America entered the 1960s in a mood of happy expectancy. John F. Kennedy had been elected president, and it seemed as if anything were possible. The Civil Rights movement was marching forward, and the humanities and arts were thriving.

There were now 85 million television sets in the United States, and the medium itself was changing. Richard Nixon and John F. Kennedy made a historic decision to broadcast their debates via television. The quiz-show scandal came to a head when Charles Van Doren was arrested for perjury in testifying that the answers to the questions on *Twenty-One* were not given in advance.

There were still plenty of variety entertainment shows on the air, and Bennett was often invited to appear as a guest. One notable occasion was Bennett's guest spot on *The Judy Garland Show*. Judy Garland found herself at a difficult point in her career. She had gained a reputation as being difficult to work with and her unpredictable behavior could make things awkward at best. By the early 1960s,

Bennett was considered by the public and critics alike to be in the same class of singers as Garland. Garland herself frequently cited Bennett as one of her favorite three singers—Frank Sinatra and Peggy Lee completing the triumvirate.

Garland's reluctance to rehearse with her guests sometimes caused the underrehearsed

musical numbers to be shaky or downright embarrassing. But despite the limited rehearsal time and the fact that they had never worked together, Garland and Bennett interacted splendidly.

Unfortunately, the folks at home tuning in to watch Bennett were not going out and buying his records. Exquisite renditions of songs from what has been called "The Great American Songbook" couldn't compete with the popular music being force-fed to the American public. By and large, popular music was at its nadir. The novelty tune "Itsy Bitsy Teenie Weenie Yellow Polka Dot Bikini" was a huge hit, while Bennett's superb recordings of "Begin the Beguine" and "The Best Is Yet to Come" were all but ignored.

Bennett's problems went beyond not being able to connect with a larger audience. His vagabond existence—he was on the road the better part of the year—was taking its toll on his family life. Bennett's wife and two sons, D'Andrea (known as Danny) and Daegal, living in New Jersey, rarely saw the peripatetic singer. In 1961, Patricia Bennett threatened Tony with divorce, the beginning of ten agonizing years of squabbling and reconciliations.

The mutual admiration Bennett and Judy Garland felt for each other is evident in this moment shared on the set of The Judy Garland Show.

Bennett had an easier time with his audiences. "It's a chemical thing with us. When I'm right, I know it by their reaction, though I can't see a thing past those lights. I feel it." Columbia Records shared Bennett's sentiments and renewed his exclusive recording contract for another five years. In a dozen years, Bennett had sold more than $16 million in records.

SECOND TIME AROUND

In 1961, Ralph Sharon and Bennett went out on tour. During an engagement at a club in Hot Springs, Arkansas, Sharon began to anticipate an upcoming date in California. It was to be the first time Bennett would perform in San Francisco, and Sharon thought it would be a good idea if they had a topical song in the repertoire. Douglass Cross and George C. Cory, Jr., who had written for Billie Holiday, presented Sharon with an eight-year-old tune that they hoped would fit the bill. The song was "I Left My Heart in San Francisco."

Despite a vote of confidence from the bartender at the Hot Springs club ("If you sing that song, I'm going to buy the record"), Bennett and Sharon had no idea that they were on to something big. At the Fairmont

JUDY GARLAND ON TONY BENNETT

Bennett and Garland, both from Queens, New York, had great affection and esteem for each other. Bennett referred to Garland as "the greatest singer this business has known." In an interview with Willis Conover, Garland gave Bennett the following encomiums:

"I think the world needs Tony Bennett as much as I need to hear him. He was born to take people's troubles away, even for an hour. He loves doing it. He's a giver."

"He is a Tony Bennett, and there isn't any resemblance to anyone else. There's just one, and everybody had better appreciate him."

Hotel in San Francisco, the reception to the song was very upbeat. Bennett, encouraged by the response, was ready to put the song on record. In January 1962, Bennett went back into the studio with Marty Manning.

The airwaves were commandeered by simplistic tunes directed at the teeny-bopper set, such as "The Lion Sleeps Tonight," "Big Girls Don't Cry," and "Surfin' Safari." It is remarkable that "I Left My Heart in San Francisco" pushed past the competition and made its way onto the charts. Music critic Will Friedwald rates "San Francisco" as "a good, though hardly great, tune and words." While "San Francisco" may not live up to the musical and lyrical splendor of a Gershwin or Porter song, it is Bennett's commitment to the lyric and emotional connection that sells the song.

In an interview with Robert L. Doerschuk, the singer recalled one of the few memories of his father, who told Bennett as a young boy that "there are only two real cities in the United States: New York and San Francisco." Bennett suggests that this psychological association of his father with San Francisco has something to do with the way he sings the song—expressing a wistfulness and loss. "I

A satisfied Bennett commands an hour-long one-man show for ABC television.

"IT IS VERY RARE IN POPULAR MUSIC FOR AN ARTIST OVER A LONG PERIOD OF TIME TO HAVE REMAINED TRUE TO HIMSELF AND KEPT GROWING WITHIN THAT INTEGRITY. TONY BENNETT IS SUCH A RARITY."
—NAT HENTOFF

always had a kind of sadness that I didn't have a father. I guess that got into the feeling of the recording." The highest position the song attained was number nineteen, but missing the top ten did little to diminish the effect "San Francisco" would have on listeners and on Bennett's career.

The appeal of the song extended well beyond the city by the bay. "San Francisco" won Grammy Awards for Best Solo Vocal Performance (Male) and Record of the Year, and stayed on the charts for two and a half years. On the basis of this song, Bennett's stature was raised to that of international superstar. Invitations to perform came from the world over.

As a result of the success of "San Francisco," Bennett opened his first one-man show at Carnegie Hall in New York

COMMAND PERFORMANCE

Pomp and pageantry are generally what comes to mind when one thinks of a command performance, not a semantic foray into the theater of the absurd. In a conversation with Earl Wilson, Bennett recounted the following exchange:

"We did a command performance, before Count Basie played for all of us. I said to Prince Philip, 'Duke, I'd like you to meet the Count.' Prince Philip said to the Count, 'Count, what do you think of the Duke?' The Count said, 'Duke, what duke do you mean?' The duke said, 'The Duke of Ellington.' The Count said, 'Oh, Duke, I didn't know you meant that duke. Why, man, that duke, he's the boss!' "

An association that bore many fruits, the singer and the pianist performed together for a ninety-minute PBS special, "Bennett and Basie Together!"

in June 1962. For the performance, Bennett assembled his greatest hits. The audience overflowed into the streets as two thousand would-be ticket buyers were turned away from a concert that had sold out two weeks earlier. Bennett cites this concert as a pivotal moment in his career. "Before, I was always playing in clubs. We did a record of that night. It was fantastic the way people cheered. I said to myself, 'That's it.' It was like going to heaven." This concert is also notable in that it was the first enormously successful concert by a nonclassical singer at Carnegie Hall. From the concert, Columbia Records released a two-record set, *Tony Bennett at Carnegie Hall,* which went on to become a best-seller.

"THERE ARE VERY, VERY FEW SINGERS I ASK THE GREAT MUSICIANS IN MY BAND TO PLAY BEHIND, AND TONY IS ONE OF THEM. BUT YOU KNOW WHAT? WHEN WE PLAY WITH TONY, WE'RE NOT BEHIND HIM AT ALL! TONY PUTS US ALL UP FRONT WITH HIM! SOMEDAY I'M GOING TO FIND A WAY TO SIT IN THE AUDIENCE AND WATCH TONY WORK WITH THE BASIE BAND, JUST LIKE A FAN. BECAUSE THAT'S WHAT I AM."
—COUNT BASIE

The song was having a positive effect on San Francisco as well. In appreciation, July 9, 1962, was declared "Tony Bennett Day." Mayor George Christopher staged an elaborate ceremony in which Bennett was presented with the key to the city and a lifetime pass for the tollgate of the Golden Gate Bridge. Bennett's worldwide bookings were so numerous that three years passed before he was able to return to San Francisco.

WORLD-CLASS ENTERTAINER

Around the world, Bennett was performing in front of capacity audiences. In England, Bennett had the honor of giving a number of command performances (performances given upon the request of royalty). Upon his return to the United States, Bennett appeared on virtually every variety television show. No longer would he have to perform in hole-in-the-wall clubs. He was now invited to appear in the tonier nightspots, such as New York's

THE COUNT AND ZEN

Jazz pianist Count Basie worked with Bennett throughout his career. When Bennett asked the master musician if he should try rock, Basie's answer resembled a Zen koan: "Why change an apple?"

Bennett was no stranger to Eastern philosophy. Louise Nevelson, the Russian-born American sculptor, had once counseled Bennett, "Just study a little Zen at night. You don't have to become fanatical about it, but it calms you down so you can rest."

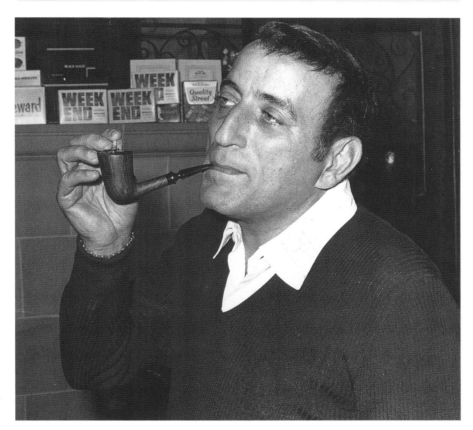

A regular cigarette smoker, Bennett sampled some pipe tobacco while in England.

Copacabana, Las Vegas' Dunes Hotel, and Miami's Fontainebleau.

Notoriety did have its drawbacks. Performing at the Cork Club in Houston, Bennett came down with a severe case of laryngitis. Despite doctor's orders not to work at all, Bennett completed his first show and ten songs of his second show before his voice gave out. That same evening, Bennett visited blind pianist Bobby Doyle, who was performing with a trio at a small jazz club. Doyle asked Bennett if he would sing "I Left my Heart in San Francisco." Bennett complied. Consequently, Glenn McCarthy, the owner of the Cork Club, charged Bennett with "walking out." Bennett countered, "If singing one number is what Glenn McCarthy calls 'doing a free show,' I guess the hour or more I usually do in my nightclub engagements is something he'd call a World's Fair exhibition." Bennett's protests aside, this act of kindness resulted in a $25,000 judgment against him.

"HE'S A BIG
BEAUTIFUL MAN.
WITH ALL OF HIS
GREATNESS, HIS HAT
SIZE NEVER NEEDED
TO BE LARGER THAN
HIS ARTISTIC
STATURE. HE'S
TOTALLY UNSELFISH,
IN A WAY COMPLETELY
UNIQUE IN THE
THEATER. TWO EXAM-
PLES: WHEN HE
BROUGHT BANDS TO
WORK WITH HIM AND
BILLED THEIR NAMES,
COUNT BASIE AND
DUKE ELLINGTON,
OVER HIS OWN
NAME. THIS IS
UNHEARD OF."

—DUKE ELLINGTON

The high potentate of jazz royalty, Duke Ellington, acknowledges Bennett's
musical accomplishments on the television special "The Best on Record."

HOLLYWOOD CALLS

Bennett's popularity continued to climb. In 1963, "The Good Life" and "I Wanna Be Around" were on the charts. The latter received a Grammy nomination for Best Vocal Performance. The Grammy committee nominated Bennett in this category again in 1964 for "Who Can I Turn To (When Nobody Needs Me)," and in 1965 for "The Shadow of Your Smile." The adulation encouraged Bennett to take the next step as a performer—acting.

Count Basie, with whom Bennett had performed a series of concerts, exhibited an uncanny ability to predict the course of Bennett's career. According to Bennett, "As I stood in the wings to watch his performance, he walked past me to go on stage and dropped this little note: 'You should do a picture.' Nothing else.

"About six months later, we were appearing on *The Andy Williams Show* together, and the only words he spoke to me that night were: 'This is the one.'"

Basie's cryptic remark was right on the money. Watching *The Andy Williams Show* that evening were producer Clarence Greene and director Russell Rouse, who were in the process of casting a feature film, *The Oscar*. When they saw the natural warmth that Bennett was able to convey on a television screen, the filmmakers instantly thought of casting him in the role of Hymie Kelly. They immediately contacted Bennett to see if he would be interested. The answer was yes.

Bennett was flown out to California for a screen test, which he passed with flying colors—the role was his. Until this point, Bennett had turned down numerous film offers in which he was to play a singer. At last, Bennett was to have the opportunity to perform a dramatic role.

Support for Bennett was coming in from everywhere. In *Life* magazine, Bennett received the highest praise imaginable from a seemingly unlikely source—Frank Sinatra, who declared, "For my money, Tony Bennett is the best singer in the business, the best exponent of a song. He excites me when I watch him—he moves me. He's the singer who gets across what the composer has in mind, and probably a little more. There's a feeling in back of it." The impact of Sinatra's statement took a while to register. In an interview with Hedda Hopper, Bennett acknowledged eternal gratitude to Sinatra and also confided, "I'm sure his mention is what brought me to Paramount and a role in *The Oscar*."

The release of *The Oscar* was surrounded by Hollywood hype. As part of the elaborate promotion, a black-tie affair saluting the film was held at the Riviera in Las Vegas, where Bennett was scheduled to open in the hotel's Versailles Room. The film's stars and studio executives attended the festivities, which were hosted by Mike Douglas and filmed for his syndicated television show. The $2.1 million film, supported by

At the premiere of <u>The Oscar</u>, Stephen Boyd, Elke Sommer, and Bennett seem unsure as to which camera they should address or ignore.

a $750,000 advertising campaign, was being given the royal send-off (even the press attended in dinner jackets). Bennett, who was hired on at $30,000 a week for his stint at the Riviera, coyly addressed those assembled: "After making a film all summer, it's good to be in a saloon where you can relax."

The Oscar premiered at Santa Monica's Civic Auditorium, then the site of the annual Academy Awards. Reviews were mixed. The movie failed to launch Bennett's film career, and although he continued to receive offers, nothing substantial was ever made of Bennett the actor.

Toward the end of 1965, Bennett found himself in the doldrums. The primacy of rock music and the overwhelming popularity of The Beatles threatened to force Bennett into oblivion. For his work on *The Oscar*, Bennett would have welcomed even a fraction of the acclaim that had been bestowed upon *A Hard Day's Night* a year earlier. His marriage, which had been on somewhat shaky ground, was also in serious trouble.

In a *Life* magazine article with Robert Sullivan and Joe McNally, Bennett relates the tale of lonely Christmas Eve at the Gotham Hotel in New York City. After a decade and a half of constantly performing, thirty-nine-year-old Bennett was facing a professional and emotional crisis. Alone in his hotel room, Bennett

heard some unfamiliar sounds. Upon opening the door, he was greeted by singers from one of Duke Ellington's Sacred Concerts, who where singing "On a Clear Day You Can See Forever." The gesture was an attempt on Ellington's part to cheer up an old friend. Bennett managed to bear up and carry on.

In the middle of one of the worst blizzards in New York history, Bennett set house records at the Copacabana. Nightly, hundreds of fans weathered the storm in hopes of standing room.

In spring 1966, Bennett's return to the celebrated Cocoanut Grove was widely heralded. Bennett stated, "I don't have the voice of a Mario Lanza, and I don't look like Robert Goulet, but I love to sing. When I'm on stage singing to an

audience, I see myself with frightening clarity. I feel the reality of me. I'm living with what I am, doing what I do best, and it feels good and the audience knows it."

Rock may have eclipsed Bennett's mass-market appeal, but the veteran performer still packed plenty of commercial clout. In 1966, Bennett's records were selling at a rate of eleven thousand a day in the United States. "San Francisco" continued to sell one thousand copies a week after four years.

On television, the Singer Sewing Machine Company sponsored a one-hour ABC television special entitled "Tony Bennett." The director of the show, Dwight Hemion, was familiar with Bennett's work—fourteen years earlier, he was camera director for *The Steve Allen Show* when Bennett guested. Hemion was also on the production staff when Bennett took over as Perry Como's summer replacement, and was already responsible for two very successful television specials featuring popular singers—Frank Sinatra and Barbra Streisand.

"Tony Bennett" was a huge commercial and critical success. Television reviewer Don Page praised Hemion as "a genius at selecting talent" and suggested that the show could have been subtitled "Artistry."

Bennett surveys London from above. The statue of Admiral Nelson in Trafalgar Square rises in the near distance.

In North America, the demonstrative audiences of screaming, hormonally out-of-control girls who once flocked to Bennett were now focusing their attention on The Beatles and the Rolling Stones. In Europe, Bennett was greeted with the type of furor that greeted the English rock groups in America.

Bennett returned to the home front in late 1967 after an extremely successful tour of Europe with the Count Basie Orchestra. The experience had a very positive effect on Bennett. In an interview with Leonard Feather, Bennett announced, "I have arrived at a point where I don't want to make any concessions just to get ahead. I could very easily get into trouble sales-wise, but I'm sorry, I can't do a song unless I feel it. I want to stay with the great songwriting specialists, the Jimmy Van Heusens, the Johnny Mercers, the Harold Arlens. I'm moving more and more toward music, rather than having a company dictate to me. I feel a great audacity toward these IBM

I ALMOST LOST MY LIFE IN SAN FRANCISCO

Most of the taping for the "Tony Bennett" television special was done in the studio. One segment, however, featuring "I Left My Heart in San Francisco," involved location shots in and around San Francisco. One setup required Bennett to sing while standing on a rock along the Pacific coast.

"I told Dwight Hemion that the waves looked pretty big to me and he said not to worry, it was low tide. Then suddenly, a huge wave came along and knocked me flat. It almost took me out to sea. On the program, of course, it will look funny, but I got banged up pretty good."

Tony poses on the Pacific coast, out of his usual attire and dressed in the flashier fashion of the late sixties.

machines that tell me, 'This is how we want you to do it, whether you like it or not.' I don't know how long I can get away with it, but it's fun. It's a funny thing. The better the songs I record, the more people seem to like it."

Bennett was able to "get away with it" for only a few more years. Columbia Records continued to exert pressure to do surefire hit songs. Bennett resisted. After all, Bennett's drawing power was stronger than ever. Contrary to Columbia's impression of its artist's popularity (or lack thereof), Caesar's Palace in Las Vegas recognized the singer's broad appeal and signed Bennett to a lifetime contract. A luncheon held to announce the pact was attended by more than a hundred disc jockeys, hotel executives, and, yes, Columbia Records honchos.

In 1969, Bennett was on the road thirty-seven weeks, averaging two shows a night. A month or two was spent fulfilling recording-studio obligations. In a conversation with Phil Casey, regarding

CIVIL RIGHTS

excessive dedication to work, Bennett testified. "I believe a man's life is his work. I used to lay off a month or two, and I'd get nervous, insecure. Laying off makes me restless.... I like to keep up the tempo of my life. I think work is the answer to a lot of things."

Professionally, work provided the answers. Personally, work asked the questions. On September 25, 1969, Patricia Bennett sued her husband of seventeen years for divorce on grounds of adultery and desertion. The suit charged that forty-three-year-old Bennett had committed adultery with Sandra Grant, a singer, in an apartment in Manhattan on New Year's Eve 1966 and "in the months and years before and after that date." Grant was pregnant with Bennett's baby. Patricia Bennett charged that her husband left her as early as August 19, 1964, and "willfully, continuously, and obstinately" deserted her. As part of the suit, she asked for custody of their two children. The marriage, which had been on the rocks for most of the decade, was dashed to pieces and would ultimately end in 1971 after a drawn-out legal battle.

Curiously, two days earlier, while Bennett was being presented with a bronze medallion by

Bennett was able to break away from personal engagements and problems to become a part of a crucial moment in the Civil Rights movement. Bennett marched with Dr. Martin Luther King, Jr., in the historic Selma–Montgomery march in 1965, which culminated with a rally of 50,000 people at the Alabama capital. (Years later, Bennett was asked to play himself in a miniseries documenting King's legacy.) The march was organized to protest the denial of voting rights to blacks attempting to register to vote.

Bennett was persuaded to join the protest by Harry Belafonte, who told him the true extent of the horror and brutality. Jimmie Lee Jackson, a twenty-six-year-old black civil rights demonstrator, had been savagely murdered.

Bennett, one of the few white performers willing to associate himself with Civil Rights causes, recalled a scene of tragic irony. When Bennett was asked to perform in the middle of a rainy night in Selma, a stage was constructed out of the most abundant material available—coffins, donated by an undertaker.

Bennett believes that we "must open our hearts and all be committed to one another instead of walking away from one another."

Mayor Lindsay of New York City at City Hall Plaza, a small group of women invaded the marriage license bureau in the Municipal Building across the street, protesting the "unholy state of matrimony." If the prophetic irony of the situation were not enough, the women proceeded to descend upon Mayor Lindsay and present him with a list of grievances as Bennett sang "I Can't Give You Anything But Love."

For Bennett, things had a peculiar way of balancing out. It was as if his personal and professional lives were somehow bound up in a self-contained hydraulic system. Traumatic domestic events were countered by wonderful career moments. During the Apollo 10 mission, in which the lunar module was brought within 9.4 miles (15km) of the moon's surface, the astronauts were awakened one day to the strains of Bennett's recording of "The Best Is Yet to Come." The song was chosen because the lyrics include "You think you've flown before—but you ain't left the ground." In the liner notes to the Columbia-released box set, Bennett succinctly states, "Now, that was...far out!"

As the decade came to an end, Bennett found himself in a precarious situation, one that appeared to mirror his plight ten years earlier. Constant touring ensured that his records sold well enough, but rock 'n' roll and the new acid-rock ruled the day. Years on the road had been the undoing of his marriage, and another long-term relationship was falling apart: Columbia Records and Tony Bennett were about to part company.

SOME
OTHER
TIME

Bennett favors large orchestral settings. Here he rocks in front of a full string section. Curiously, the Big Band Era, which ended with the ascendency of solo artists, has occasionally been revived by singing stars such as Bennett.

From 1960 to 1970, the American spirit went from a condition of joyful anticipation to woeful disenchantment. The United States was firmly entrenched in the Vietnam War, and after two years, the Paris peace talks hadn't made any progress. At Kent State University in Ohio, four students who had been protesting the war were killed by the National Guard. The generation gap had widened into a chasm.

Toward the end of the sixties, Bennett made great efforts to attract the younger generation, going so far as to insist on special matinee performances for teenagers during engagements in Chicago and New York. The theater managers feared there would be no audience or, worse, mobs of unruly teenagers. Bennett's belief that given the chance, the younger crowd would respond favorably to his music, was vindicated.

In both cities, he performed before well-behaved, appreciative capacity crowds. Onstage, Bennett was a giant; on vinyl, he was being dwarfed.

Bennett's audience consisted primarily of an older generation, and consequently the number of his fans was dwindling. Although Bennett's live performances continued to fill halls around the world, there was no direct

Time to relax and survey a book has always been a luxury rare and treasured by the extremely busy Bennett.

correlation in record sales. From the mid-sixties on, Bennett's record sales were relatively stable, selling in moderate volume. Columbia Records, however, wanted enormous sales. The youth of the day appeared more interested in acquiring the "now" sounds of rock and protest music. Bennett stood by his credo that performance was at the heart of selling records and that talent would win in the end.

The sad truth was that promotion was the key, and without it even the most gifted musical genius would be condemned to obscurity. Twenty years earlier, the star-making technicians at Columbia were happy to give Bennett the big push—their fledgling artist was in sync with the prevailing musical tastes. By the late sixties, Columbia was less inclined to foist what it considered an old act on a new public.

The record industry had changed drastically in the past two decades. The philosophy of record sales was driven more by the marketing department than by artistic vision. Rather than diversify their musical product, the executives, especially Columbia's president, Clive Davis, aimed to pinpoint the current trends in popular music. The next step was to conscript the Columbia roster of artists to record only material that the trends in the market demanded. Generally, this exercise in philistinism failed to revive lagging sales and succeeded only in vitiating the artists' work.

To the adolescent, Bennett's recordings of "then" music, no matter how good, seemed out of touch, even irrelevant. "It was a tough time then for singers of standards. Many succumbed to the pressure from their record labels. Not Tony. He refused to make concessions." This was Rosemary Clooney's (not entirely correct) assessment of the situation. In concert, Bennett

made an effort to work some current hits of the day into his repertoire. In accord with his artistic modus operandi to live and work with songs before committing them to record in the studio, Bennett endeavored to warm up to this alien material over time. This effort was due largely to Davis' continued pressure for an album that would appeal to the youth market. The results were a somewhat hastily recorded album entitled *Tony Sings the Great Hits of Today*, released nine days before the new decade.

HIT OR MISS

Had Bennett conceded? Well, yes and no. In his own way, Bennett had courted the "now"-music hordes by selecting songs from the current popular scene that he thought would have the same enduring appeal as his "evergreen" selections. Instead of churning out an unimaginative cover version, Bennett endeavored to stamp the songs as his own by choosing offbeat arrangements and altering the tempo of the familiar product—anything to justify the decision to go against his personal aesthetic. The results varied, and Bennett was literally sickened by the project—vomiting before the recording session. By robbing Bennett of his artistic dignity,

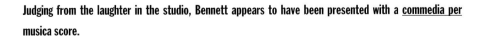

Judging from the laughter in the studio, Bennett appears to have been presented with a <u>commedia per musica</u> score.

Davis had won a Pyrrhic victory—an album was gained, but the artist was lost.

The departure from the standards and venture into the foreign territory of contemporary hits provides insight into the heart and soul of Bennett as a singer. Bennett may not have the distinctive phrasing and swagger of a Sinatra or the velvet euphony of a Mel Tormé, but nobody can match Bennett for ingenuousness. Bennett's style is entirely devoid of irony. What comes across is a candor, sensitivity, and charm, which have led critics to designate him "Mr. Lovable," "Mr. Sincerity," and "Dr. Feelgood," among other such appellations.

Sinatra's panegyric declaring Bennett the "best singer" and "best exponent of a song" is far from hyperbole. As William Butler Yeats asks in the final line of his poem "Among School Children," "How can we know the dancer from the dance?" in Bennett's case one must ponder, "How can we know the singer from the song?" When Bennett is in good form, his embodiment of the song, his complete surrender to the material, allows for an event in which the listener experiences a merging of art and artist. While other singers may be more proficient craftsmen or greater masters of technique, Bennett's singing tran-

scends easy analysis. Bennett is the song, and the song is Bennett.

On the *Great Hits* album, an uncharacteristic rift between the singer and the song was apparent. Of course, not all the contemporary pop music was execrable. Bennett was content with his choice to record certain songs from the rock canon. For example, Bennett personally selected "Something," which Frank Sinatra called "one of the greatest love songs ever written," composed by George Harrison of The Beatles, to be included in the four-disc collection, providing a forty-year overview of his career. Contrary to Davis' idiot notion, the album of "hits" did little to generate interest from die-hard rock fans for whom Bennett's

versions were nothing more than novelties. If anything, Bennett was in danger of losing the remainder of his core audience.

In the loss category, things were decidedly less than pleasant in the Bennett marriage. In February, Patricia Bennett indicated that Bennett, fed up with the tediousness of the divorce proceedings, had been quoted as saying he would pursue a Mexican divorce. Bennett's estranged wife reacted by procuring a New Jersey court order that restrained Bennett from obtaining a divorce outside of the state.

Meanwhile, Bennett was engaged in other skirmishes. The music of the early seventies reflected the great dissatisfaction and anger of America's youth. Bennett attacked the "angry lyrics" as "positively obscene" and decried, "I'm fighting for the FCC to step in with a much stronger hand to censor more of the rock 'n' roll radio stations." Frustrated, Bennett was lashing out at a system that promoted so-called message music and ignored what Bennett termed "beautiful songs about love." At the time, Bennett proclaimed, "Great songs and big bands go together. I wouldn't feel comfortable singing a great song with a three- or five-piece band of electronic instruments. I feel today's

The Chairman of the Board grants an audience to the Bennetts during a soiree at the Beverly Hilton Hotel in 1975.

PICKING UP THE PIECES

screeching, electronic sounds hurt the ears, whereas the sound of the big bands caressed them."

Bennett's situation was paradoxical. The Big Band Era ended around 1949 as the changing economics of the road made touring with a large number of musicians financially unfeasible. The decline of the Big Band gave rise to the career of the solo vocalist (e.g., Bennett, Clooney, Sinatra) as the main attraction. However, Bennett, who recorded and performed in both small and large musical settings, was not arguing to bring back the Big Band Era: he was expressing instead his anxiety over the dissonance of the sonic product that was being purveyed as music. Bennett seemed concerned about the far-reaching effects of the music and feared the violent lyrics would beget violent behavior.

Although Bennett's beliefs were far from "hip," they were grounded by sincerity and integrity. Bennett championed what appeared to be a dying tradition. Toward the end of 1970, Bennett shot a pilot for a musical television series with Twentieth Century

In May 1972, Bennett performed at the induction ceremony for the Songwriters Hall of Fame. Before an audience of six hundred, Bennett sang "I Want to Be Around to Pick Up the Pieces When Somebody's Breaking Your Heart." Given Bennett's romantic situation at the time, it is interesting to note the origin of this song.

Sadie G. Vimmerstedt of Youngstown, Ohio, a retired cosmetician, was responsible for the song's title. Upon reading that Frank Sinatra had married Ava Gardner, Vimmerstedt thought these words summed up how Sinatra's wife, Nancy, must have felt and scribbled them in pencil on a "dirty old piece of paper."

Vimmerstedt ultimately sent the phrase to composer/lyricist Johnny Mercer, known to her only through his records. Mercer, taken with the title, wrote words and music to go with it and included Vimmerstedt as coauthor, giving her a 50 percent cut of the royalties. At the ceremony in which Bennett sang her song, Vimmerstedt, who received an average of $3,000 a year for her effort, laughingly remarked "I'm no songwriter."

Fox. Bennett challenged the status quo, which required a modern approach and designed the series as a television version of the old *Chesterfield Supper Club* radio show. The public was not feeling terribly nostalgic and the show went no further.

NOT-SO-FOND ADIEUS

At Columbia Records, things had reached critical mass. Despite evidence that Bennett singing hits of the day sold no better than Bennett singing standards, the pressure was still on to listen to the call of demographics—not the muse. Bennett was given the ultimatum that if he refused to record what Columbia dictated, he would be let go. Bennett responded, "Let me go." Columbia brass wanted Bennett to do Janis Joplin. Bennett rejoined, "You do it." Thus, a twenty-two-year relationship that produced more than eighty albums, numerous hit singles, and millions of dollars was ended. (Columbia managed to release seven more Bennett albums after his departure.) Bennett entered the third decade of his career without a major record-label contract.

Bennett's personal life was on the same roller-coaster track as his recording career. On the downside, in December 1971, Patricia Bennett was granted a divorce after nineteen

"ANYBODY WHO CAN MAKE HIT RECORDS OUT OF GOOD MUSIC NOWADAYS HAS GOT TO BE AN EXCEPTIONAL PERFORMER. IN TONY'S CASE, I APPRECIATE THE DIMENSION THAT MOST OTHER SINGERS DON'T HAVE. THE THIRD DIMENSION: TRUTH."
—HERBIE MANN

years of marriage. In the divorce settlement. Bennett was required to surrender his $150.000 Englewood. New Jersey, home. to give up custody of his children. and to pay $92.500 a year in alimony and child support. On the upside, in a secret ceremony in London on December 29, Bennett married Sandra Grant. his companion of five years and mother of his two-year-old daughter. Joanna. Addressing the issue of his new romantic partnership. Bennett announced. "I am by nature a shy man. and it was occasionally a source of embarrassment that Sandi and I were not married."

DESERT DRAW

The early seventies were a period of transition for popular music. Although rock was considered to have lost its hard core. MOR performers such as Bennett. Vic Damone, and Perry Como still had to find a home for their acts. That home. nestled in the Nevada desert, was Las Vegas. In an interview in *Billboard*. Bennett asserted. "Las Vegas is the most important place to work in the world. If you play even a third-rate spot in Vegas, then in Europe you're a big star. Everywhere in

Europe. Las Vegas is looked upon as the place to play. If you've played Vegas, then in Europe you have it made."

Bennett knew whereof he spoke. In February 1972. Bennett's Festival Hall concert in London set a new record when it sold out in thirty-five minutes. During a provincial tour of Britain in the same year. Bennett's engagements were all standing room only—a remarkable feat in that other American acts. expected to generate big ticket sales, failed miserably at the time. Bennett told Roger Watkins of *Variety*, "Britain provides me with moral sustenance. The audiences are receptive

and appreciative. They respond to quality material. and I get a real uplift from playing here. I don't get the same feeling anywhere else in the world. I'm morally recharged. I feel I've managed to improve a little as a performer. I go back home with renewed professional confidence."

The morally revived and artistically enriched Bennett returned to Las Vegas in the spring of 1972 and signed an eighteen-month contract as a headliner at the Las Vegas Hilton. The contract required six weeks of appearances at $100.000 per week. Bennett thought that Europeans

respected and appreciated his art. whereas Las Vegas audiences represented an exercise in art depreciation. Clearly, the audiences in Vegas had more on their agenda than merely savoring a Bennett performance. The purpose of a headliner like Bennett was to draw the right kind of clientele. In essence. Bennett's shows were a diversion from the real matter at hand—gambling. Bennett summed up his carriage-trade following: "They are the people with money. the kind of clients who, for instance, the casinos want to attract. People who think nothing of dropping $25.000–30.000 at the tables after the show."

ABOVE: Bennett performed in Las Vegas nearly as regularly as these showgirls. OPPOSITE: Once again, Bennett is flanked by showgirls. Playing in Las Vegas often paved the way for performers to appear at such London venues as the Paladium, where Tony posed backstage.

It is a testament to Bennett's talent and appeal that he was considered a big draw in Vegas, which was widely recognized as a "tough" town. Although he was quite aware that his Vegas audiences might be more concerned with casino activities other than his performance, Bennett still cared greatly about the success of his engagements. During an eleven-day engagement at the Hilton in May, Bennett spent more than $20,000 of personal funds for radio, newspaper, and billboard advertisements. In a wide-scale promotional effort, more than two hundred of his albums were given away in radio contests. In the three weeks before Bennett's September engagement at the Hilton, he ran daily newspaper notices heralding his triumphant return. Bennett's manager at the time, Derek Boulton, clearly had an impact in making the singer more publicity-conscious. Bennett was coming to terms with promotion. It was all very good indeed to have phenomenal talent, but Bennett now realized that you had to let the people know it was there. Besides, good audience turnout ensured future, extremely lucrative engagements at venues on the Las Vegas Strip.

SHOWMANSHIP

Around this time, Bennett's stage show took the form that it would have for the better part of the seventies. First, the taped voice of Frank Sinatra would introduce the singer. Then, although Bennett was usually opposed to gimmickry in his shows, he did augment the evening's repertoire with an extra element—film. While Bennett performed "I Left

My Heart in San Francisco," images of the San Francisco area were projected, and accompanying "Smile" was footage of the song's composer, Charlie Chaplin. Unlike the rock shows of the era, which literally incorporated smoke and mirrors, Bennett's shows used these multimedia effects as a complement to, not a distraction from, the music. Music critic Leonard Feather put it best when he proclaimed, "If I ruled the world I would summon every overnight millionaire pop/rock singer to spend a full evening listening to Tony Bennett with the simple admonition: 'Study!'"

Also in 1972, the city of San Francisco, in appreciation of what Bennett's recording of "San Francisco" had done for the city, attempted to present Bennett with an antiquated cable car. One wonders what possible use Bennett could have had for such a white elephant of a gift. Bennett found a unique way of declining: "I asked the mayor what time the ceremony took place and he told me that it was in the morning. I told him that I was sorry but I never got up that early." Presumably, one who left his heart in San Francisco preferred to leave the cable cars there as well.

"TONY BENNETT'S GREAT BECAUSE HE SINGS LYRICS WITH THE DEEP PERSONAL CONCERN OF A FOLK SINGER WHO BRINGS OUT THE TRUE MEANING OF A SONG." —BARBRA STREISAND

ABOVE: The modern recording studio is ideally suited to a singer of Bennett's talent. Advanced recording techniques can capture every nuance of the singer's vocal dynamic—from a powerful fortissimo to a delicate pianissimo. OPPOSITE: Bennett's emotional dedication to a song is nonpareil. With only a microphone, free of any gimmicks, he is able to distill the purest essence of a musical piece.

Despite his claim of not being an early riser, Bennett, at age forty-six, still maintained a schedule that would exhaust those half his age—on the road approximately thirty-four weeks of the year, working on television and movie projects, and cutting two record albums a year. Happily, Bennett was back in the recording studio. Bennett had set up a distribution deal with MGM Records. Unlike Columbia, MGM gave Bennett free artistic rein. Bennett was permitted to produce his own records, which MGM agreed to distribute. On October 12, MGM kicked off a major promotion of Bennett's initial offering on the label when the singer opened at the Fairmont in San Francisco. Bennett's first album for MGM, *The Good Things in Life*, delivered what the title promised. The artist was allowed to follow his muse, and the result is a superior recording of Bennett singing standards. MGM even allowed Bennett to provide artwork, in the form of one of his paintings, for the album. Bennett's association with MGM lasted a little over a year. Drastic company cutbacks forced MGM and Bennett to part ways in the autumn of 1973.

During this period, Bennett caught the attention of the great Italian film director Vittorio DeSica. Francis Ford Coppola's motion picture *The Godfather*, a huge critical and financial success, had done little to enhance the image of the Italian community. In an interview with Donald Zec, Bennett acknowledged his distress over gossip linking him with the Mafia. Bennett remarked, "Look, a guy runs into every type in cabaret. You can't identify every Joe who wants to shake your hand….It's only the average bigot who says to you: 'Hey, you Italian—Mafia, huh?'" DeSica wanted to use Bennett's life as a paradigm to show "another view" of the Italian-American experience. A script, tentatively titled *Two Bits*, was developed based on Bennett's life as a performer, but the project never came to fruition. But the failure of the project had little effect on Bennett, who continued to burgeon as a performer.

If the last years at Columbia represented a time when Bennett was being manipulated by the powers that be, then 1973 marked a year in which the artist took firm control of his career. Bennett was doing what he wanted to do and singing what he wanted to sing. Bennett had the financial and artistic clout to call the shots. During an engagement at the Las Vegas Hilton, Bennett's act called for 103 symphonic musicians (flown in from as far away as Hawaii) to accompany him onstage. Stringent Las Vegas musicians' union rules required that an additional 103 local musicians be retained to stand by. Bennett's drawing power was so great that the Hilton unflinchingly hired the 206 musicians. In the early seventies, there were few artists with the authority to singlehandedly command a Big Band setting—that is, until the summer of 1973.

On April 29, 1973, the musical dynamic shifted dramatically when Frank Sinatra announced that he was ending his "retirement." Ever gracious, Bennett welcomed the competition: "It's good for all of us that he's coming back because it will be like the thirties, when there was a spirit of healthy competitiveness. Everyone sings better when Frank's around." Freed from the constraints of Columbia's three-album-a-year schedule of prescribed material and facing the challenge of Sinatra, Bennett was singing better than ever. The creative juices were flowing, and Bennett's talent as a graphic artist was revealed to the public at an exhibition at Lincoln Center in New York, where his works were displayed along with those of other celebrity painters. Bennett proclaimed, "Everybody should do two things at a time. So I sing and paint."

In April 1974, Bennett, again under the sure direction of Dwight Hemion, filmed a television special in London that paired him with Lena Horne. The production, "Tony and Lena," aired in the United States in September and received stellar reviews. *New York Times* television critic John J. O'Connor commented, "The hour is consistently pleasant, frequently superb. Both singers are, of course, master stylists, possessors of musical taste and distinctive phrasing. And that is precisely, and intelligently, the focus of the programs. There is no patter, no cute routines, no nonsense." The no-nonsense program, embraced by the public, gave rise to an extensive North American tour for the two performers that lasted well into 1975.

OPPOSITE: Bennett welcomes the fabulous Lena Horne onto the stage for their ABC television special, "Tony and Lena." The warm regard these two major talents share for one another is undeniable.

Although almost a decade had passed since Bennett's participation in Dr. Martin Luther King, Jr.'s historic march for civil rights, there was ample evidence that race relations were less than ideal in the United States. In October 1974, the hotbed of social unrest was not the Deep South but the Northeast, specifically Boston. In May, Bennett had been awarded an honorary doctorate of music at the Berklee College of Music in the same city. Now, five months later, the disquiet over the busing of school-children had reached such a fevered pitch that black children were being stoned and black citizens were being beaten. Horne could not bring herself to perform the concerts scheduled at Boston's Symphony Hall and formally cited the racial situation as cause for cancellation. Bennett once again revealed his integrity and agreed to cancel the shows. Both Bennett and Horne absorbed the expenses for the cancellation.

THE BEST IN THE WEST

On April 6, 1974, another daughter, Antonia, was born to the Bennetts. Shortly thereafter, Bennett, Sandi, and their two daughters moved into a house in Beverly Hills. The 5,800-square-foot (539 sq m) house, built in 1911, was remodeled and included five bedrooms, a maid's quarters, a guest house, and a pool house converted into a music/painting

Bennett and Lena Horne's musical association, which was initiated in London, lasted for more than a year and filled theaters throughout North America.

studio. The change of atmosphere seemed to agree with Bennett, who acclimated quickly to the West Coast.

During his time in Los Angeles, Bennett made a number of gestures to indicate his commitment to his new city. In addition to a variety of benefit concerts to support local causes, Bennett offered Mayor Bradley of Los Angeles a tape of his recording of "Life Is Beautiful" to be considered as Los Angeles' official city song. The official song at the time, "Angel Town," had limited appeal with Los Angelenos and was popular only among fans of the Angels baseball team— located in Anaheim! Bennett campaigned hard for his song, but the mayor was bothered that Los Angeles was not mentioned in the song. Cannily, Bennett pointed out that the United States is not mentioned in the national anthem. Bradley was not convinced and Bennett was never given a chance to do for Los Angeles what he had done for San Francisco.

Surely, Bennett's efforts could hardly be viewed as an entirely altruistic contribution to the City of Angels. It must be noted that Bennett had just formed his own record label, Improv Records, and that "Life Is Beautiful," written by Fred Astaire, was the title song of

the first album for the fledgling company. Over the next few years, Bennett and his business partner, Bill Hassett, owner of the Statler Hotel in Buffalo, would struggle to make Improv a financially viable company. As part of their corporate plan, the Downtown Club in the Statler was revived. This venue served as the location for live concerts that were recorded for release by the label.

Improv Records offered some of the finest jazz recordings of the early seventies. Bennett had recorded an album for Fantasy Records with Bill Evans, who, as part of a reciprocal agreement, would record an album for Improv. In addition to Bennett's pop-jazz stylings with Bill Evans, jazz greats Earl "Fatha" Hines, Marian McPartland, and

Charlie Byrd were part of the small label's catalog. But Bennett's network of twenty-three distributors in the United States, with RCA helping out in Canada, were unable to generate good sales volume. Bennett's admirable, if doomed, corporate philosophy was, "We are not so much interested in huge unit sales as we are in presenting good music to the public." The public was all but indifferent to the Improv merchandise, and the label, consistently in the red, was forced to fold.

As if in response to the public's seeming apathy, Bennett observed, "I'm a slow starter and study long. But it's worth it, because when I hit it, I hit it right and it lasts. My songs are still selling as well as they did in 1950." Nobody would have disputed Bennett's claim about his marksmanship as a singer, but lacking the distribution and promotion provided by a huge corporate entity such as Columbia Records, Improv was bound to fail. Ironically, it was the Columbia catalog of Bennett songs that maintained any respectable sales volume.

In an interview with *Time*, Bennett referred to himself as "just a saloon singer." By the

The Bennett family—(from left to right) Joanna, Tony, Sandi, and Antonia—enjoy some quality time together and review some very important paperwork.

mid-seventies, Bennett's "saloons" included the Royal Albert Hall, the Waldorf-Astoria, and the White House—locales hardly evoked in the song "One for My Baby." Eventually, Bennett would appear onstage with the man who all but defined the "saloon singer." On the night of July 27, 1975, as part of Gower Champion's tribute to Ira Gershwin, Bennett and Sinatra shared the stage at another "saloon"—the Dorothy Chandler Pavilion of Los Angeles' Music Center.

The following July, Bennett returned to the toniest of venues, Carnegie Hall, to open the twenty-third Newport Jazz Festival. The audience responded favorably to Bennett's performance, but the presence of a pop singer at a jazz festival raised some eyebrows and a few tempers. During Bennett's act, a voice from the audience demanded, "This is supposed to be a jazz festival. Bring back Bill Evans!" Jazz pianist Bill Evans had accompanied Bennett earlier in the evening. In his *New York Times* review of the concert, John S. Wilson noted, "It was Mr. Bennett's evening and he made the most of it. He was in good voice, strong and sure, pacing his program with a skill that he has mastered brilliantly. He is a superb old-fashioned pop singer."

TONY BENEFIT

Bennett had spent a quarter-century as an entertainer. Among his life experiences were hit records; sold-out concerts; radio, television, and

Tony Bennett surely did not leave all of his heart in San Francisco. He saved a big part of it to share with others across the country.

As Chairman of United Way's "To the People" campaign, Tony is bringing a United Way message of people helping people to millions through the magic of his music, the warmth of his smile and his commitment to serving people the United Way.

United Way

TONY BENNETT is National Chairman of United Way's "To the People" campaign. Don't miss United Way's new theme song "There's Always Tomorrow."

film successes; two marriages and four children; his share of drugs, depression, and time on the psychiatrist's couch; and worldwide name recognition. In November 1976, billed as one of the nation's "living national treasures," Bennett performed at the Smithsonian Institution before a sold-out audience. Even though Bennett's sales as a recording artist were slight at this time, his concert career was solid. The performer's second marriage, subject to the strains of his constant touring, appeared to be holding up. Although his life in general was fairly stable, Bennett felt something was missing—charity.

Years earlier, Judy Garland had urged Bennett to "go out and help everybody. You'll feel better for it." At the time, Bennett made some excuse as to why he could not. When he finally heeded Garland's advice, Bennett remarked, "Whenever I've gone out to help

people, I have felt better." Bennett's involvement in a variety of causes became so extensive that he earned the nickname "Tony Benefit."

In addition to myriad acts of generosity, Bennett committed himself as national spokesman for the United Way for its 1976–1977 campaign. Bennett, not content to be employed as a mere figurehead for the philanthropic organization, became actively involved in its "To the People" communications program. In a television spot, Bennett earnestly declared what could be considered his philosophy of caring: "We all have personal problems; there are some things we can't handle by ourselves. Sometime in your life you have to reach out to help or be helped. Perhaps that's the greatest thing we do as human beings—touch each other."

In May 1977, the ever grateful city of San Francisco again paid tribute to its favorite crooner. Mayor George Moscone officiated at the dedication of Tony Bennett Plaza (the courtyard of the Mark Hopkins Hotel on Nob Hill), and in Golden Gate Heights a street was named Tony Bennett Terrace. As a visual artist, Bennett was validated by his first one-man show in Chicago. It was a positive time for Bennett. Life, love, and career were going well, but tragedy was just around the corner.

On Thanksgiving night, 1977, Anna Benedetto died. Bennett kept the news of his mother's death a secret from his fans until the end of his Sunday performance. Bennett

As spokesman for the United Way, Bennett is depicted before the Golden Gate Bridge. Given the incredible success of Bennett's recording of "I Left My Heart in San Francisco," the image of the singer paired with the bridge has attained iconic status in popular culture.

announced. "She was a great lady and would have wanted it that way. And I wouldn't have wanted to disappoint the audiences." Bennett may have worn the brave face of a trooper, but he was devastated. Bennett's feelings over his mother's demise ran deep. Having retired his mother twenty-five years earlier in a house purchased with the earnings from "Because of You" was a curse of sorts. Bennett recalls, "When she was working, she was healthy. The minute she stopped, she fell apart." When she died, Bennett fell apart. Months of depression ensued, and Bennett admits, "I thought it was the end of me....I went crazy."

Bennett slowly healed, but the road ahead appeared rocky. His mother had been the one constant in his sometimes tempestuous life. Her death ultimately resulted in an unanticipated nine-year hiatus from the recording studio. Bennett would not appear again on record until the mid-eighties.

On his gorgeous recording of "Some Other Time" with Bill Evans in 1975, Bennett conveyed a longing and pathos that the listener cannot help but feel. The resignation tinged with yearning in Bennett's delivery of the two-note lyrical phrase "Oh, well" suggests that although Bennett is not a blues singer, his experience has allowed him to move beyond the blues into a more refined, transparent, musical realm. The lyrics continue, "Just when the fun is starting/Comes the time for parting/But let's be glad/For what we've had/And what's to come." What was to come would be a renaissance for Bennett's career, but it was going to take patience, planning, and that dirty word, promotion.

Is Bennett checking for rain or is the audience merely showering him with affection?

Chapter Five

HOW DO YOU KEEP THE MUSIC PLAYING?

Although he has allowed his hair to go gray,
Bennett still conveys a youthful exuberance in

HOW DO
YOU
KEEP
THE
MUSIC
PLAYING?

76

Popular music in the late seventies was a mixed bag. The motion picture *Saturday Night Fever*, with a hit double-album soundtrack, helped disco music gain a widespread audience. On the opposite end of the spectrum of the often lavishly arranged, syrupy dance music, punk rock reared its ugly head with minimal compositions of maximum noise. As the popularity of both disco and punk declined, record-company executives rushed to label the latest crop of rock music "new wave." This meaningless term did not so much classify common musical modalities as it merely lumped together those acts that were not rock, disco, or punk. The typically myopic marketing directors presumed that it was easier to sell a product called "new wave," no matter how nebulous a designation, than promote something considered old hat. Consequently, "adult contemporary" acts, such as Bennett's, hardly figured

In performance, Bennett sings with a commitment matched by few vocalists. His involvement is, in the words of the great jazz standard, Body and Soul.

BENNETT THE ARTIST

Throughout the years, Bennett continued to pursue his talents as a painter, signing his works with his given name, Anthony Benedetto. During the lull in his recording career, Bennett found more time to dedicate to this avocation. Appearances on The Tonight Show with Johnny Carson allowed Bennett a forum in which to display his art to the vast public and consequently generated interest among gallery owners.

Bennett became so serious about this alternative career that he made an effort to paint every day and constantly carried a sketch pad. Studying with art instructors in New York and London, Bennett ultimately earned the praise of other artists such as David Hockney. Bennett's sketches, as well as his works in acrylic and oil, have been displayed in galleries around the world and have sold for as much as $40,000. In an interview with Leonard Feather, Bennett remarked, "The simple fact is that I like to sing and I like to paint, and I'm fortunate enough to be able to make a living doing the two things I love most."

In addition to providing Bennett with a substantial source of secondary income, painting has a therapeutic effect on the artist. Bennett confided to Claire Carter that "painting calms me and transports me to another place." Given the increased sales and rising price tag of original Benedettos over the years, perhaps that place is a higher tax bracket.

The painter and his model: at an exhibition of his work, Bennett offers a toast before a self-portrait.

into the recording industry's merchandising schemes.

Bennett was no longer recording albums, but his live performances, television appearances, painting, and benefit work kept him busy the better part of the year. In 1978, art imitated life when Bennett played himself in *King*, a six-hour NBC miniseries chronicling the life of Martin Luther King, Jr. Bennett's generosity was seemingly limitless. In addition to benefit concerts for the United Way, ailing musician friends, and individual foundations. Bennett lent his artwork to Actors and Others for Animals, a nonprofit organization dedicated to the humane treatment of animals. The sale of greeting cards bearing Bennett's oil-on-canvas depiction of a skyscraper, *40 Stories High*, helped support the organization.

Bennett's absence from the recording studio had some unforeseen benefits. In the years following Sinatra's famous remark, Bennett found himself overcompensating as a singer, as if to match the praise. The resulting oversinging did little to improve Bennett's voice or further his career. Now, liberated from the obligation to record three albums a year. Bennett was able to focus his energy on hon-

ing his craft, a task that occasionally had eluded the performer. As Bennett told Richard Harrington, "I have this ambition as a performer to try to get better as I get older…. It's my ambition to hold on to my equipment and sing well right through the years."

Trouble in Paradise

Bennett had a firm grip on his equipment, but other aspects of his life remained outside his

grasp. As early as 1976, in an interview with Marshall Berges of the *Los Angeles Times*, tension could be detected concerning Bennett's second marriage. As evidenced in her response to the seemingly innocuous question, "Are you happy?" Sandi Bennett replied, "Ask me tomorrow if you want a cheerful answer," and followed up with a catalog of woes. In comparing her life with her husband's, she remarked, "My life seems empty." However, Sandi put on a good face. Noting their love, she declared, "I like being married. It's a nice moral life, and it suits me just fine." The couple was not at loggerheads, but neither did they represent a picture of domestic bliss.

Three years later, as with Dorian Gray, the picture revealed a little more damage. Sandi Bennett alone was interviewed by Marilyn Funt for the tabloid *The National Enquirer*. At the top of this exchange. Mrs. Bennett was not feeling blue—she was seeing red. The angry spouse indicated resentment over Bennett's not taking "strong enough action to bring about divorce" from the first Mrs. Bennett. As the interview progressed, Sandi described a breakdown in communications with her husband regarding

A photogenic clan—out for the evening on the West Coast with Sandi and his two daughters.

the birth of the couple's second child. After assuring the interviewer that Bennett was very happy and loved his baby daughter, Sandi commented that his behavior was "very strange" during her pregnancy and acknowledged her own severe postpartum depression. The capper was, "I really want this marriage to survive, but it has to survive on new terms."

As the fissures began to expand in Bennett's second marriage, the singer was busy defining "terms" with another family member—his son. Danny Bennett, a rock guitarist who had fronted his own group, Quacky Duck, and later played with Neon (Bennett's other son, Daegal, played drums) took over the management of his father's career in 1979. Inasmuch as there was no shortage of people out to take advantage of a performer of Bennett's rank, it made sense to make things a family affair. Danny Bennett's first hurdle was to impress upon his father the idea that marketing could be used to the singer's advantage without compromising his dignity or aesthetics.

DANNY, BENNETT'S "TEN-YEAR PLAN"

The younger Bennett was on the right track. For years, Bennett championed great music—songs that had survived for a number of years and had not become dated or old, tunes that were ageless. Bennett was seen as one of the good guys, a man of principles, a dapper dresser (named as one of the best-dressed men of 1978 by the Fashion Foundation of America), and a class act with a superb singing voice. While Sinatra was held in awe as "The Chairman of the Board," Bennett's fans felt a kinship with the Queens crooner who had no fancy sobriquet: the man who was simply "Tony." Danny could see how these aspects of his father's personality could be distilled and disseminated to a brand-new, youthful market. All Bennett needed was the right exposure.

In addition to Bennett's usual sold-out performances

Bennett, looking quite casual in a running suit, engages in some friendly banter with the recording engineer.

around the world. Las Vegas beckoned again. Bennett earned $1.8 million for a sixteen-week engagement at the Desert Inn. However, Bennett's finances had never really been an issue. From his first hit record, Bennett had always worked, continually earning top dollar for his performances. A Vegas engagement was financially rewarding but did little to increase Bennett's visibility and presence beyond the desert. Appearances on *The Tonight Show* with Johnny Carson and Bennett's perennial television specials were the best ways for getting the performer's name across to the larger public. Bennett even guest-starred as himself, singing two songs, in a short-lived NBC series starring Karl Malden entitled *Skag*. Collections of Bennett's hit tunes issued by Columbia Records continued to sell steadily, but the Bennett camp was not out to sell albums (there being no new releases): the goal was to sell a new generation on Tony Bennett. The question remained: how was this to be done?

Again, Bennett's personal and professional lives were on the same roller-coaster track. While Bennett was trying to reach out to a new generation, the second Mrs. Bennett was reaching out on her own. In May 1980, the *Hollywood Reporter* noted that Bennett was

already involved in efforts to keep his Beverly Hills home from his estranged wife. The brief article went on to report that Sandi and Gene Kelly were an item (around this time, Bennett was seeing Michael Caine's former partner, Minda Feliciano). Years later, in an interview with Richard Goldensohn, Bennett would reflect, "I really would have liked a 'marriage made in heaven' and a good family life, but this business I'm in doesn't help that kind of thing. With all the travel involved, there's just no sense of continuity. A woman who wants to stay at home, well, she just can't be happy with someone who lives out of a suitcase."

Sandi Bennett was most evidently not happy. In addition to filing for divorce, Mrs.

Bennett had a palimony suit for the five years of togetherness prior to their marriage—a legal gambit that could have rewarded her with half of everything. During this period, Bennett moved back to New York, leaving his wife and two daughters with the use of their Beverly Hills home. Ultimately, the couple was divorced in the early eighties. The house in which Sandi lived was eventually sold as part of the couple's property settlement for just under $1.65 million in 1994 (down from the asking price of $2.75 million).

Bennett was at an impasse of sorts both personally and professionally. His second marriage was clearly coming to an end, and Bennett's self-imposed exile from the studio meant that his record-buying public was slowly evaporating. It was very difficult to find a niche for Bennett in the market of the early eighties. Bennett's critically acclaimed, artistically superior albums of the mid-seventies suffered from a lack of proper distribution. When Improv Records failed, the record industry erroneously assumed Bennett's "arty" records were not marketable. Surely there were small record labels that would have loved to sign Bennett, but the likelihood of the same distribution fate that met Improv made Bennett wary. Bennett thought it best to avoid the studio altogether rather than confirm the half-baked, simpleminded conclu-

OPPOSITE: Following a moment of vocal achievement, Bennett communicates a tremendous amount of heartfelt joy and satisfaction. **ABOVE:** With Sandi, the second Mrs. Bennett.

With Honors

In March 1981, Bennett was given the highest accolade of his career. The praise was not from fans or critics or even fellow musicians, but from those without whom he would have had no career—Bennett received a Lifetime Achievement Award from the National Academy of Popular Music, an association of songwriters. At the Annual Songwriters Hall of Fame dinner in New York, Bennett was honored by the Academy president, Sammy Cahn. Cahn decreed, "It's a valentine from the writers who are grateful to Tony for making the great songs sound even greater." Bennett responded, "It's the greatest honor I could ever receive."

Honors and tributes were bestowed upon Bennett frequently. In October 1982, Bennett was asked to be the grand marshal of the Columbus Day parade on Fifth Avenue in New York. Bennett was the third in a line of Italian entertainers who had held the position,

the two previous grand marshals being Luciano Pavarotti and Frank Sinatra. Additionally, Bennett received the Columbus Citizens Committee Humanitarian Award at the Waldorf-Astoria Hotel.

The music-listening/public was aware of Bennett, but there was a danger that engagements at the Smithsonian Institution and hon-

ors with titles such as "Lifetime Achievement" would make people perceive Bennett as a relic or museum piece, not a current, vital artist. In the early eighties, musicians and music promoters had more to do than just get their songs on the radio or make television appearances. The cable-television industry gave birth to the first network dedicated solely to popular music: MTV (Music Television) changed the way music was heard, seen, and sold. However, it was unlikely that Bennett, now in his mid-fifties, would be welcome on MTV, which marketed to teenagers and the twenty-something set. Besides, the fledgling network promoted current records, and Bennett had none to offer.

In a conversation with Leonard Feather, Bennett, bitter about the record business, attacked the foolishness of the industry's focus on youth. Bennett observed, "Now the young kids are spending more and more of their money on Atari games instead of putting it into jukeboxes or buying records. The record people would have been better off concentrating on the old Bing Crosby format of entertaining the whole family." Bennett's sensible economic theories

As grand marshal of New York City's Columbus Day parade Bennett receives a plaque bearing his likeness. The singer appears quite amused at the bas-relief rendering of his famous proboscis.

sions of record-company corporate executives.

HOW DO
YOU
KEEP
THE
MUSIC
PLAYING?

83

aside, the record industry was not about to change its decades-long practice of going after the youth market. For the meantime, popular music, and especially MTV, were for the younger crowd.

But there was always a place on television for Bennett— at PBS (Public Broadcasting System). In March 1982, *New York Times* critic Janet Maslin lauded "Bennett and Basie Together!" as a must-see musical event. The show, which featured Bennett and Basie together and separately, was described as "buoyant." Bennett was the consummate entertainer, and this ninety-minute concert revealed the singer in top form. Maslin commented that Bennett sounded "a little hoarse at that, but his performance [had] incomparable dash and energy."

San Francisco was another place where Bennett would never wear out his welcome. When the 109-year-old cable-car system was shut down for an overhaul, Mayor Diane Feinstein convinced Bennett to sing a few bars of "I Left My Heart in San Francisco." When the $60 million restoration of the transit system was complete, Bennett attended the citywide festival marking the official reopening. San Francisco's adopted native son declared, "One of the great treats in life is to ride on a cable car. The whole world has been waiting for this day." When asked if he ever got tired of singing his signature song, Bennett responded, "Do you ever get tired of making love?"

RECONCILIATION

By the summer of 1985, Bennett's sons (both Danny and Daegal were now involved in managing and producing) had apparently set up

ABOVE: Danny and Daegal, at the time in the rock group Quacky Duck & Barnyard Friends, attend their father's opening with their stepmother.

an exciting new recording deal for their father with a major label. When addressing the press, Bennett was very secretive about the details of the arrangement. Only two facts seemed clear: Bennett would have artistic control, and the album would be recorded in London.

Technology also played a part in Bennett's return to the studio—specifically the compact-disc format. According to Danny Bennett, "The CD made it possible for us to emphasize the voice, which is what made Tony a star to begin with." The prospect of a new Bennett album, after a nearly ten-year absence from the recording studio, was tantalizing, and the mystery label through which the finished product would be released was a source of great speculation.

When *The Art of Excellence* was released in May 1986, those who followed the vagaries of Bennett's recording career were stunned by the label with which the singer chose to do business: Columbia Records, the most unlikely of bedfellows, was

SAY WHAT?

Throughout the years, music critics have rushed to the thesaurus and summoned deep reserves of metaphoric invention to describe Bennett's unique voice. Herewith are a few of the adjective-rich assessments of Bennett's vocal instrument:

"Bennett's voice, however, is distinctly his own; it has a diffused No. 00–sandpaper sound."
—Time, *January 1952*

"His voice is as flat as it is strong; his timing slips and falters like a water wheel in a drought."
—Time, *March 1964*

"He has a husky, limited voice."
—John S. Wilson in the New York Times, *1970*

"Bennett's silvery supple voice is faltering somewhat these days."
—Peter Goddard in Chatelaine, *1986*

"Over the last ten years Bennett's voice has deepened, darkened, become raspy."
—Jim Miller in Newsweek, *1986*

"Tony Bennett is back where he belongs, cruising silky-voiced along the outskirts of jazz…. his voice is losing its range and authority. That said, he hasn't sounded this good in years."
—Peter Goddard in Chatelaine, *1990*

"Bennett's clarion, nasal, cozy baritone shows weathering but little fraying at sixty."
—Fred Bouchard in Downbeat, *1991*

"Tony Bennett's voice is rich and true, slightly whiskered, aged in oak."
—Howard Mandel in Audio, *1993*

"His vocal timbre has become quite husky."
—Stephen Holden in Audio, *1993*

"His voice is smooth and rich and light, like whipped butter."
—The New Yorker, *1994*

Bennett's "new" label. Behind this peculiar and unexpected alliance was Danny who masterminded a reconciliation between his father and the record company. Danny acknowledges that the secret to his success in negotiating with Columbia lay in convincing the new management that Bennett "was a catalog artist, and there was gold in them thar' hills." The younger Bennett also theorized that the resurgence in Bennett's popularity had much to do with commercially viable recordings of standards by the likes of Linda Ronstadt, Carly Simon, and Willie Nelson. Bennett's records were to be marketed as the "real thing" as opposed to the spate of "alternative" versions. After all, Bennett had been singing standards for more than thirty-five years, and no matter how earnest the recording of these tunes by Ronstadt and the others may have been, they appeared to be only students dabbling in a new form— Bennett was the master artist. Ultimately, Danny's perseverance and shrewdness garnered his father a five-album contract with Columbia with one proviso: the singer was granted complete artistic control. All aspects of production, from the recording engineer to the final mix, were completed before the albums were delivered to Columbia for pressing and distribution.

The Art of Excellence received favorable reviews and major distribution, but breaking through to the larger, record-buying public remained a marketing conundrum. In concert, Bennett clearly appealed to a wide age range. Booked at Radio City Music Hall for the first time in 1986, Bennett was thrilled to note that his audience included more young people than old. Retailers, not entirely convinced of Bennett's broad base of support, were more likely to target younger record buyers and dedicate valuable space to promotional materials for Madonna or Whitney Houston records rather than Bennett's new album. Despite attempts to create consumer awareness and interest for Bennett's new album, sales were disappointingly lackluster.

Back in the studio, Bennett produced two more albums under his new contract by the end of the decade: *Bennett/ Berlin*, featuring tunes composed by Irving Berlin, and *Astoria*, a collection of songs meant to evoke nostalgia for the singer's hometown. Again, critical acclaim did little to sell Bennett's album. So daunted was Bennett by the inability to generate greater interest or sales that he seriously considered ending his career as a recording artist.

In a world that often considered the core of Bennett's songbook out of style, prospects seemed bleak for the die-hard proponent of the standards. Francis Davis, writing for *The Atlantic*, crystallized Bennett's predicament thusly: "Bennett has become the best singer of his kind, but he must sometimes feel like an ambassador from a country that's fallen off the map." Remarkably, this man without a country was about to chart new territory and begin the third—and greatest—resurgence of his singing career.

TOP: Although Bennett's chair-straddling was reminiscent of Marlene Dietrich, the Berlin referred to on this album cover was not the German city but the American composer Irving Berlin. ABOVE: *The Art of Excellence* marked Bennett's return to the recording studio and his reconciliation with Columbia Records. PAGES 86–87: Bennett displayed a decidedly debonair dishabille for renowed celebrity photographer Annie Leibovitz.

"HE'S A GREAT BALLADEER. HE HAS WHAT IT TAKES: THE MECHANICS, A GREAT VOICE, GOOD TASTE, AN ORIGINAL SOUND. HIS PHRASING IS RIGHT. HE IS ONE OF THE GREAT SINGERS—THE WAY A GREAT INSTRUMENTALIST IS A GREAT SINGER."
—GIL EVANS

STEPPIN' OUT

During the thirty-sixth annual Grammy Awards at Radio City Music Hall, Bennett indicates what his fans have known all along—he's number one.

In the spring of 1989, Bennett met with Don Ienner, the new president of Columbia Records, and intimated his intentions of leaving the label and possibly giving up on recording altogether because of the discouraging sales of his last three albums. Unlike those of Columbia's previous management, Ienner did not suggest that Bennett change his act and do something trendy in order to tap into the current market. Instead, Ienner implored Bennett to stay with the label and requested that the singer develop a "concept" album: something that remained true to Bennett's repertoire but that was easily marketed.

Bennett returned to Ienner with a simple two-word phrase: *Perfectly Frank*. In an interview with David Blum, Ienner remarks, "I got it right away. Some people thought he meant something about being honest. I knew he meant Sinatra." What Bennett proposed was an entire album consisting of the "torch and saloon songs" of Sinatra. Bennett's brilliant concept, which would not be realized until 1992, would serve as a tribute to Sinatra.

In the meantime, Danny Bennett was increasing his father's visibility by diversifying his television and radio appearances. In the mid-to late eighties, in addition to *The Tonight Show*, Bennett appeared a number of times on David Letterman's late-night television show, which was popular with younger television viewers. Letterman's musical director, Paul Schaeffer, served as accompanist for Bennett on these occasions. The association of the guileless Bennett with the often sardonic Schaeffer helped to create an aura of "coolness" or "hipness" around the older crooner.

Under his son's direction, Bennett made guest appearances on other youth-oriented television, such as *SCTV* and Howard Stern's short-lived WOR television show. Bennett even challenged formatted radio by going on the air on a rock station. In 1991, Bennett was invited to do a singing voice-over for *The Simpsons*, a popular animated weekly situation comedy. Danny Bennett negotiated with the producer, Jay Kogen, and the writers, Ken Levine and David Isaccs, to rewrite the episode. Originally, Bennett was only to be heard singing "Capital City"—in the cartoon universe, a song (not unlike "San Francisco") of local interest to the metropolis bearing the same name. The revised script incorporated an animated "personal appearance" by Bennett. The device succeeded in winning Bennett a new audience and began a series of celebrity guest "appearances" on the show.

ABOVE: Bennett and his son Danny enjoy the festivities at a pre-Grammy party thrown by Arista Records.
OPPOSITE: Bennett's praise for his audiences almost matches their adulation. When Bennett sings love songs, love seems to fill the room.

A collection of eighty-seven songs covering the singer's forty-year career was released in 1991. Unlike the standard compendium of greatest-selling hits that is generally represented by such sets, the songs on *Forty Years: The Artistry of Tony Bennett* were personally selected by Bennett. The singer celebrated the release of his career retrospective by performing a Fourth of July concert on the Capitol lawn in Washington, D.C. To ensure the definitive nature of this boxed set, Bennett spent seven months culling the songs from his numerous albums and provided annotations for all the tracks. Regarding the inclusion of certain tunes versus others, Bennett commented, "A long while ago, the great musicologist and composer Alec Wilder told me that to be really timeless you have to hit the direct center of the bull's-eye, so that's how I chose the songs. Some others were more popular, but I left those out if they sounded like they were a little off on the perimeter. I made sure every note hit." Once again, Bennett revealed the subtle iconoclast within. His concept of what defined a "hit" record was more in line with an archer trained in Zen than a Madison Avenue executive with an eye on yen.

RELATIVE TEMPERATURE— HOT OR COOL?

Danny Bennett's efforts were paying off. By the end of 1991, major publications, as well as Bennett's new fans, agreed that the veteran performer was "cool." The connotation of "cool" has so varied throughout the years that the meaning is elusive. The confusion about what is cool is apparent in Susan Korones Gilford's *Cosmopolitan* magazine piece, "Red Hot Right Now," which paradoxically concludes that Bennett is "very cool." Bennett certainly was not cool in the stereotypical manner of self-involved musicians who regularly seem unaware of their audiences. *New York Times* columnist Trip Gabriel noted that Bennett "has all the hallmarks of classic cool," a combination of unforced charisma, and a vocal style that is "controlled, suggesting banked passions." Gabriel supported his assessment by arguing that Bennett, unlike "hot" musicians, "has never been known to rip off his shirt." Of course, Bennett's style of "cool" is able to communicate more with the sly unknotting of a bow tie than the crazed display of a rock 'n' roller lost in the throes of ecdysis.

A full two years before the newly packaged Bennett acquired cool status, Will Friedwald wrote of Bennett's persona in the sixties: "He may have championed what became known as the 'establishment,' but as far as the basic values that the younger generation supposedly stood for, simplicity, cre-

STEPPIN' OUT
93

OPPOSITE: Bennett studied the artful use of the microphone by watching the master, Sinatra. Sometimes, in performance, the crooner clutches the microphone almost reverentially. ABOVE: A candid moment at the fifty-third Golden Globe film awards—one of the few awards with which the singer has not been honored.

Attending a variety of awards ceremonies requires a vast wardrobe. Bennett looks as elegant in white as he does in black.

ative integrity, and sincerity, Bennett made even the hippies and folkies of Haight-Ashbury look like Hollywood lawyers." Three decades later, Elvis Costello, who hit the music scene in the late seventies with an angry young man's cool disdain of his audience (Costello has since mellowed), concurred with Friedwald's pronouncement.

After singing a duet with Bennett, the awestruck Costello summed up the classic crooner's renewed popularity with the young set: "Make no mistake, this is not about kitsch but about a singer who's emotional and sincere, and that's the truest kind of style. He was modern to begin with, and the rest of us are just catching up."

FRANKLY PERFECT

With his career gaining new momentum, Bennett proceeded to record the promised *Perfectly Frank* concept album in 1992. Unlike Bennett's two previous records, *Bennett/Berlin* and *Astoria* (highly conceptual

At a taping of "Evening at Pops," Bennett was accompanied by his musical partner of more than three decades, pianist and hit finder Ralph Sharon. PAGES 96–97: Arms held wide, Bennett accepts a welcome ovation. In concert, Bennett's genial spirit conveys a warm embrace to the audience.

albums that failed to capture the record-buying public's interest). *Perfectly Frank* was a huge critical and commercial success. In Sullivan and McNally's portrait of Bennett for *Life* magazine. deejay Dick Golden maintained that Bennett's performances on *Perfectly Frank* were remarkable in that the singer delivered definitive recordings of these very familiar tunes. In Golden's words. "He's nailing these songs to the wall." Bennett had accomplished the seemingly impossible task of taking songs closely associated with Sinatra and making them his own. The very success of such a venture could only have been achieved by an artist of Bennett's stature and talent.

Regarding Sinatra. Bennett told *Time*. "He's given us the most mature popular music ever written." Bennett also acknowledged. "He doubled my audience. Sinatra's always been warm and wonderful to me." As chronicled in Friedwald's *Jazz Singing*.

despite a friendly competition between the two crooners. Sinatra consistently exhibited a sense of fair play. going so far as to recall his single of Bennett's "San Francisco" shortly after its pressing. The wide appeal of this "concept" album helped Bennett's tribute to Sinatra become his biggest-selling album in thirty years. Bennett would have to recheck his computation as to Sinatra's multiplicative effect on his audience. *Perfectly Frank* quickly sold 500.000 units. earning Bennett his first gold record since *I Left My Heart in San Francisco.*

Reviewer Howard Mandel appraised Bennett's efforts in the *New York Times*: "Bennett seems to live every turn of phrase by the likes of Porter. Gershwin. Rodgers. Mercer. and Arlen. Even with such keynotes in place. it's remarkable the singer so completely infuses warmth into an homage to the symbol of cool cynicism. the man Bennett calls 'King of the Entertainment World.' To be perfectly frank. forget about Sinatra and know

ABOVE: Regular guy Bennett rides in the front seat of a taxi and seems to offer a positive review of the ride. OPPOSITE: Upon the release of *Forty Years: The Artistry of Tony Bennett*, the singer assisted the promotional campaign. At music retailer Sam Goody, Bennett stood before a promotional placard.

that the monarch of lounge bel canto wears his crown too modestly." In addition to high accolades and phenomenal sales, the album earned Bennett a Grammy Award. Bennett's career had caught a wave that was rapidly turning into a tsunami.

Bennett followed the success of *Perfectly Frank* with *Steppin' Out*, a homage to the great song-and-dance man Fred Astaire, who died in 1987. In paying tribute to Astaire, Bennett provided evidence that he was not out merely to turn a quick buck by attaching an easily recognized name to his latest project. It is most certain that Bennett's newly won audience was bound to find the name Astaire (who was out of the entertainment scene by the late seventies—before many of Bennett's youthful fans were born) less familiar than that of Sinatra. *Steppin' Out*, a collection of impeccable recordings in which Bennett distills the essence of Astaire's elegance through his singular delivery, was another landmark for the mature singer. The popularity of *Steppin' Out* provided Bennett with the rare distinc-

tion of winning back-to-back Grammy Awards, this time for Best Traditional Vocal Performance.

Curiously, Bennett's extensive renaissance enabled him to repay his debt to the original

saloon singer. In addition to propelling Bennett's career into the stratosphere, *Perfectly Frank* paved the way for Sinatra's *Duets*, a hugely popular 1993 collection of Sinatra standards sung with current popular recording artists. Although *Duets* went platinum, the quality of the production fell shy of Bennett's recordings. In fact, Sinatra himself did not actually sing with his partners—the "duets" were accomplished through the technical wizardry of combining vocal tracks recorded at different times, often in other cities. In an interview with David Blum, Columbia Records president Don Ienner commented, "I think Sinatra's people said to him, 'Look at Tony Bennett. He's making an album with your songs, and it's a hit.' So Frank turns around and makes *Duets*. It does well. They spend a fortune to market it. But *Duets* is not a good album." As Bennett had noted years earlier, when Sinatra was doing well, there was a reciprocity throughout the world of the standard singer. It was time for Bennett to complete his "crossover."

TOP: Bennett was supported in his promotion of *Perfectly Frank* by his two lovely daughters. **ABOVE:** Bennett and his beautiful companion, Susan Crow. The two met at a concert in the late 1980s and have been together ever since.

Dressed to match the cover of his Grammy Award—winning album *Perfectly Frank*, Bennett got into the marketing groove and helped move the recording that put the singer back on the charts.

Backstage at the 1993 MTV Video Music Awards, Bennett is flanked by Flea and Anthony Kiedis of the Red
Hot Chili Peppers, thus closing the supposed generation gap.

I Want My MTV

In 1993, Bennett appeared as a presenter at the MTV Video Music Awards. Joining Bennett on stage were members of the popular rock group Red Hot Chili Peppers. In a sartorial role reversal, Anthony Kiedis and Flea, of the Chili Peppers, appeared in formal evening dress, while Bennett donned sunglasses and the casual garb of the younger generation. In a bit of scripted silliness, Bennett pretended to interrupt his copresenters with an oddball attempt at their radio hit "Give It Away." Bennett succeeded in displaying a sense of humor about himself and won over the MTV crowd.

The Bennett–Chili Pepper alliance was the crucial cornerstone in building Bennett's presence on MTV. A black-and-white video of "Steppin' Out with My Baby" (the title track of Bennett's Astaire tribute) made its way onto MTV as a "buzz clip," a spot usually reserved for the "alternative" music of the flannel-clad grunge set. Yet what could be more "alternative" to a generation of listeners who believed Seattle was the center of the music universe than Tony Bennett?

In 1994, MTV offered Bennett a shot at its popular *Unplugged* series. The *"unplugged"* setting purported to present rock acts such as Eric Clapton, Bob Dylan, and Nirvana in a stripped-down, free-from-studio-trickery format. Bennett commented to Jancee Dunn in *Rolling Stone*, "They call it 'unplugged,' but

Bennett and chanteuse k.d. lang reprised their <u>Unplugged</u> duet of "Moonglow" at the thirty-seventh annual Grammy Awards in 1995.

I've been acoustical for years, you know?" For Bennett's *Unplugged* appearance, the singer and the Ralph Sharon Trio were joined by Elvis Costello, k.d. lang, J. Mascis of Dinosaur Jr., and Evan Dando of The Lemonheads. At the conclusion of his rendition of "Fly Me to the Moon," Bennett revealed the true meaning of the term "unplugged": using a crowd-pleasing device the performer had employed as the finale to his stage performances for years, Bennett turned off his microphone and sang the last three words, "I love you," as a declaration of his affection to the audience. After a standing ovation, an emotional Bennett declared, "This has been one of the most wonderful nights of my life."

Songs from Bennett's *Unplugged* performance made up Bennett's next album, which won Album of the Year honors at the 1995 Grammy Awards. Bennett immediately followed up his MTV concert with an appearance on *Modern Rock Live*, a syndicated radio talk show, and went on to perform in concert with rock acts like The Lemonheads, Porno for Pyros, Teenage Fanclub, and Belly.

Danny Bennett was named as one of the top one hundred marketers of 1994 by *Advertising Age* in recognition of his revival of his father's career. Things were going very well for the senior Bennett—for the first time in years, his professional and personal lives were on the ascendant. Bennett was happily romantically involved with Susan Crow (near-

ly forty years his junior), a manager of jazz musicians, and his popularity was the highest it had ever been.

Bennett's fame was so pervasive that it seemed as if the singer were likely to appear just about anywhere. The excitement attendant on Bennett's half-time performance at the Super Bowl easily eclipsed that of the previous year's act, self-named King of Pop Michael Jackson. Bennett had become so firmly ensconced as a popular American icon that actor/filmmaker Albert Brooks sought to recruit the singer to perform the national anthem in his baseball comedy, *The Scout*. Bennett was reluctant; at first believing he was being mocked, Bennett expressed a disinclination to "sing songs that glorify war." Ultimately, Bennett was won over, and Brooks declared, "I'm more proud of getting Tony than anything, but I'm exhausted."

Bennett, who was anything but exhausted, continued to perform more than two hundred dates a year. As a celebrity endorser, Bennett exceeded the affiliations of professional athletes. Among Bennett's commercial liaisons

OPPOSITE: Bennett appears in formal evening wear so often that it's difficult to imagine the entertainer dressed otherwise. ABOVE: Once again, the musical generations come together. At a 1995 MusiCares dinner in his honor, Bennett socialized with David Crosby of Crosby, Stills & Nash.

are credit cards. dairy products. sugar substitutes. and computer software companies. Bennett remained idealistic. donating much of his advertising fees to charitable foundations.

The year 1995 found the Bennett juggernaut practically unstoppable. On both coasts. the singer was honored. as Los Angeles. San Francisco. and New York celebrated "Tony Bennett Day." MusiCares honored Bennett as Person of the Year. In Monaco. Prince Albert presented Bennett with two World Music Awards. one for best-selling jazz album of 1994. and the other for his lifelong contribution to the music industry. Late in the year. Bennett released yet another "concept" album. *Here's to the Ladies*. a tribute to the great female vocalists. In addition to his usual television appearances. Bennett taped a television

ABOVE: Bennett employs a unique impromptu exercise regimen—multiple repetitions with a pair of gleaming Grammy Awards. The nineties have offered the singer ample opportunity to heft numerous awards. **OPPOSITE:** Bennett introduces the MTV generation to the "Great American Songbook" during his <u>Unplugged</u> appearance.

special to tie in with his latest collection of tunes. As opposed to the album, which showcases Bennett singing solo, the CBS special "Tony Bennett: Here's to the Ladies" featured the crooner singing duets with a variety of female entertainers, including Liza Minnelli, Patti Labelle, and comedienne Rosanne (who, as a singer, is infamous for her regrettable rendition of the national anthem).

THE BEST IS YET TO COME

As of 1996, Bennett's popularity was at an all-time high. Bennett's ability as a singer had never been more refined. If the performer's career once seemed like a harrowing roller-coaster ride, it now appeared to be a gentle ascent to ever greater heights. In the first few months of the year, in addition to the talk-show circuit,

Bennett performed a live Valentine's Day special on the Arts & Entertainment network, in which the singer, accompanied by the Ralph Sharon Trio, took requests phoned in to a toll-free number. Further proof that Bennett's appeal knows no bounds was evidenced by Bennett's welcome appearances on shows ranging from PBS's sublimely sophisticated Charlie Rose to ABC's ridiculously raucous Muppets Tonight.

The secret to Bennett's longevity is best explained by the singer himself: "Through song and art, I can communicate what I believe is the essence of life—truth and beauty. In my time, I've seen both go out of style, but they always come back in vogue again....It's not just that I want to sing, I have to. The heroes of my life, Duke Ellington, Basie, and Fred Astaire, they just kept working until the day they died. So will I."

ABOVE: Both Rosanne and Bennett are actively involved in humanitarian causes. Bennett's television special "Tony Bennett: Here's to the Ladies" featured the popular comedienne. OPPOSITE: From a New York City photo shoot for Bennett's television special Tony Bennett Live by Request: A Valentines Special. PAGE 110: Bennett takes a breath as his audience hangs in eager anticipation for the crooner's next musical statement. PAGE 111: Bennett's joyful exuberance is testament to his profound love for his work. Well into the fifth decade of his career, the singer's excitement remains genuine and infectious.

BIBLIOGRAPHY

Arnold, Denis, ed. *The New Oxford Companion to Music*. New York: Oxford University Press, 1983.

Balliett, Whitney. *American Singers: Twenty-Seven Portraits in Song*. New York: Oxford University Press, 1988.

Beck, Marilyn. "Tony Bennett Hits at 'Obscene Rock.'" *Citizen News*, July 29, 1970.

Bellafante, Ginia, "People." *Time*, September 14, 1992.

Bennett, Tony. "Tony Tells His Fortissimo Views." Citizen-News, July 26, 1968.

———. *Reflections*. Sony Music Entertainment, New York, 1991.

Berges, Marshall. "Home Q & A." *The Los Angeles Times*, August 22, 1976.

"Biography of Tony Bennett" (film). *Paramount Pictures*, September, 1965.

Blackwood, Nina. "Tony Bennett: A Man For All Seasons, A Man For All Times." *Cyberpop.com*, 1995.

Bleeden, Joe. "Truly Timeless Tony Bennett Goes 'Unplugged.'" *Senior Highlights*, June 1995.

Blum, David. "The Cooling of Tony Bennett." *New York*, August 22, 1994.

Bouchard, Fred. "A Winning Kinda Guy." *Down Beat*, October 1991.

Brown, Lester C. *Les Brown's Encyclopedia of Television* (third edition). Gale Research, Inc., Michigan, 1992.

"Caesars Palace Pacts Tony Bennett for Life." *Variety*, July 14, 1969.

Carter, Claire. "'Our Love Was Strong.'" *Parade Magazine*, February 16, 1992.

Cateura, Linda Brandi. *Growing Up Italian*. New York: William Morrow and Company, Inc., 1987.

Cities of the United States, Second Edition, Volume 4: The Northeast. Michigan: Gale Research, Inc., 1990.

Clark, Alfred L. "Five Women Protest the 'Slavery' of Marriage." *The New York Times*, September 24, 1969.

Clarke, Donald, ed. *The Penguin Encyclopedia of Popular Music*. London: The Penguin Group, 1989.

Columbia Records Biography, August 1963.

Conover, Willis. "20 Years With Tony." *Billboard*, November 30, 1968.

Daly, John. "Reaping the Tony Awards." *Macleans*, August 1, 1994.

———. "Tony Bennett: Better Than Ever." *The Saturday Evening Post*, January/February 1995.

Davis, Francis. "The Real Stuff in Life." *The Atlantic*, August 1990.

Doerschuk, Robert L. "Halfway to the Stars." *San Francisco Focus*, November 1992.

Dumpert, Hazel-Dawn. "Ladie's Night." *L.A. Weekly*, November 24, 1995.

Dunn, Jancee. "Tony Bennett." *Rolling Stone*, April 7, 1994.

Ebert, Alan. "He Keeps Coming Back Like A Song." *Good Housekeeping*, April 1995.

———. "Bennett Finds Room for Improv." *Los Angeles Times*, September 28, 1975.

———. "The Unchanging Tony Bennett." *The Los Angeles Times*, September 5, 1982.

———. "Bennett Satisfied With Music, Art, Offspring." *Los Angeles Times*, August 27, 1985.

Fink, Michael. "Tony Bennett is Still Upbeat About His Career." *L.A. Herald Examiner*, September 10, 1982.

Flippo, Chet. "On the Town With Tony Bennett." *New York*, May 11, 1981.

Friedwald, Will. *Jazz Singing*. New York: Charles Scribner's Sons, 1990.

———. *Sinatra! The Song is You: A Singer's Art*. New York: Scribner, 1995.

Gabriel, Trip. "Cool Is Back." *The New York Times*, June 12, 1994.

Gavin, John. "Tony Bennett Carries the Torch for Classic Pop." *The New York Times*, September 27, 1992.

Giddins, Gary. "The One and Only Frank Sinatra." *Stereo Review*, February 1984.

Gifford, Susan Korones. "Red Hot Right Now." *Cosmopolitan*, August 1991.

Giles, Jeff. "Queens Crooner Makes Good." *Interview*, May 1990.

Goddard, Peter. "Crooners of a Certain Age." *Chatelaine*, March 1986.

———. "Astoria: Portrait of the Artist." *Chatelaine*, June 1990.

Goldensohn, Richard. "Tony Bennett: The Other Saloon Singer." *Attenzione*, September 1980.

Graham, Judith, ed.. *Current Biography*. New York: The H.W. Wilson Company, 1995.

Grobel, Lawrence. "Eternally Hip." *TV Guide*, May 28, 1994.

Grun, Bernard. *The Timetables of History*. New York: Simon & Schuster/Touchstone, 1991.

Harrington, Richard. "Tony Bennett, With Heart." *Washington Post*, July 9, 1985.

Haskins, James. *Lena: A Personal and Professional Biography of Lena Horne*. New York: Stein and Day, 1984.

Heisler, Gregory. "Frank & Co." *Life*, December 1990.

Hopper, Hedda. "Bennett: He Sings, He Acts." *Los Angles Times*, October 1965.

Hunt, Dennis. "Tony Bennett Leaves His Art to His Public." *Los Angeles Times*, March 18, 1975.

"Idol of the Girls." *Time*, January 14, 1952.

Jones IV, James T. "Tony Bennett's Heartfelt 'Artistry.'" *USA Today*, July 2, 1991.

Kart, Larry. "They Can't Take Away Tony Bennett's Trademark: The Fine Art of Feeling." *Chicago Tribune*, July 13, 1986.

King, Susan. "The Benefits of Being Tony Bennett." *Los Angeles Times*, November 26, 1995.

Kirsch, Bob. "Tony Bennett & Partner Seek Quality In New Label." *Billboard*, November 8, 1975.

Lanza, Joseph. "Maker of Smooth Music." *Pulse*, December 1995.

Larkin, Colin, ed. *The Guiness Encyclopedia of Popular Music*, New York: Stockton Press, 1992.

Levin, Eric. "After a Decade Off the Records and On the Road, Tony Bennett Makes His Richest Disc Ever." *People Weekly*, June 23, 1986.

Lieberman, Frank H. "Tony Bennett Ponders Song Writing." Herald-Examiner, July 3, 1971.

Low, David. *Fodor's New York City*. New York: Fodor's Travel Publications, Inc., 1993.

Mandel, Howard. "Pefectly Frank." *Audio*, January 1993.

Marchese, John. "When He Croons, Slackers Listen." *The New York Times*, May 1, 1994.

The Merrick Company Press Release, April 28, 1966.

Miller, Jim. "Crooning To a New Generation." *Newsweek*, September 8, 1986.

Milward, John. "Tony, Tony? Tony!" *The Los Angeles Times*, April 15, 1994.

O'Connor, John J. "TV: A.B.C. Teams Bennett and Lena Horne at 9." *The New York Times*, September 9, 1973.

————. "Tony Bennett and MTV: Talk About Bedfellows." *The New York Times*, June 1, 1994.

"'Oscar'-Winner Junket Attending Tony Bennett Las Vegas Opening." *Variety*, September 23, 1965.

Page, Don. "ABC One-Hour Show 'Tony Bennett.'" *Los Angeles Times*, October 28, 1966.

Perry, Patrick. "Talking With Tony." *The Saturday Evening Post*, January/February 1995.

Rosenthal, A.M. *World of New York*. New York: The New York Times Company, 1985.

Ryon, Ruth. "Hot Property." *Los Angeles Times*, November 28, 1993.

Sadie, Stanley, ed. *The New Grove Dictionary of Music and Musicians*. London: Macmillan, 1980.

"The Saloon Singer." *Time*, Janauary 13, 1973.

Schapp, Phil. *An Earlier Bird*. New York: Polygram Records, 1988.

Scott, John L. "Vegas Wild Over Bennett." *Los Angeles Times*, October 9, 1965.

Shalett, Mike. "On Target." *Billboard*, June 7, 1986.

Shipman, David. *Judy Garland: The Secret Life of an American Legend*. New York: Hyperion, 1993.

Simon, George T. *The Best of the Music Makers*, New York: Doubleday & Company, Inc., 1979.

Smith, Joe. *Off The Record: An Oral History of Popular Music*. New York: Warner Books, Inc., 1988.

Schwartz, Jonathan. "The Best G.D. Pop Singer I've Ever Heard." *GQ*, October 1990.

Sullivan, Robert, and Joe McNally. "Tony Bennett: Older and Wiser." *Life*, February 1995.

Swartz, Jon D. *Handbook of Old-Time Radio*. Lanham, Md., The Scarecrow Press, 1993.

Thibeau, Alice. "The Crooner and the Cable Cars." *San Francisco*, June 1984.

"Tony and His Song." *Newsweek*, October 1, 1951.

"Tony Bennett." *TV Guide*, June 20, 1959.

"Tony Bennett, In the Mix." *The New Yorker*, April 25, 1994.

"Tony Bennett Tells Why He Marched with Dr. King in Selma." *Jet*, April 6, 1992.

"Tony's Second Time Around." *Time*, March 6, 1964.

"3 Old Pros, Tony, Vic & Perry Improve MOR's Image." *Billboard*, November 4, 1972.

Various. *Billboard.* 2/6/71, 9/23/72, 3/11/95, 5/13/95.

Various. *Hollywood Reporter.* 7/14/69, 9/22/69, 5/5/ 72, 5/24/74, 5/23/80, 7/29/81, 8/31/81, 1/23/87, 4/24/87.

Various. *L.A. Herald-Examiner.* 6/29/69, 10/3/69, 7/20/63, 2/21/72, 3/13/75.

Various. *Los Angeles Times.* 8/7/67, 9/19/69, 2/15/70, 9/1/72, 9/16/73, 7/3/75, 8/28/77 11/29/77, 3/6/81, 9/22/81.

Various. *National Enquirer.* 7/24/79.

Various. *The New York Times.* 5/17/72, 11/16/76, 3/5/82, 3/11/82, 7/4/91.

Various. *Newsweek.* 1/17/72.

Various. *People.* 10/17/94.

Various. *Time.* 12/13/71, 7/2/84.

Various. *TV Guide.* 1/30/88.

Various. *Variety.* 12/11/63, 2/16/73, 12/22/76.

Wilson, John S. "Tony Bennett Shines at Philharmonic." *The New York Times.* September 28, 1970.

———. "Jazz Festival Is Opened By a Superb Pop Singer." *The New York Times.* June 27, 1976.

The World Book Encyclopedia. Worldbook, Inc., Chicago, 1994.

Zec, Donald. *Some Enchanted Egos.* New York: St. Martin's Press, 1973.

SELECTED DISCOGRAPHY

Throughout Bennett's recording career, especially during his initial tenure at Columbia Records, the singer's songs have been mixed and matched in a seemingly endless variety of compilations. The purpose of the following discography is to provide a list of those albums (33 1/3 LPs and compact discs) which truly represent unique collections of Bennett tunes. Unfortunately, the majority of Bennett's early recordings are out of print and have not yet been collected and issued on compact disc.

1955
Cloud 7 (Columbia)
Alone At Last with Tony Bennett (10", Columiba)

1956
Because of You (10", Columbia)

1957
Tony (Columbia)
The Beat of My Heart (Columbia)

1958
Long Ago and Far Away (Columbia)
Tony's Greatest Hits (Columbia)

1958
Basie Swings—Bennett Sings (Roulette)

1959
Blue Velvet (Columbia)
If I Ruled the World (Columbia)
Alone At Last with Tony Bennett (Columbia)
Because of You (Columbia)
Tony Bennett In Person! (Columbia)
Hometown, My Town (Columbia)

1960
To My Wonderful One (Columbia)
Tony Sings for Two (Columbia)
Alone Together (Columbia)
Tony Bennett Sings a String of Harold Arlen (Columbia)

1961
My Heart Sings (Columbia)
Bennett and Basie Strike Up the Band (Roulette)

1962
Mr. Broadway: Tony's Greatest Broadway Hits (Columbia)
I Left My Heart In San Francisco (Columbia)
On the Glory Road (Columbia)
Tony Bennett At Carnegie Hall (Columbia)

1963
I Wanna Be Around (Columbia)
This Is All I Ask (Columbia)

1963
Fascinatin' Rhythm (Sunbeam)

1964
The Many Moods of Tony (Columbia)
When Lights Are Low (Columbia)
Who Can I Turn To (Columbia)

1965
If I Ruled The World: Songs For The Jet Set (Columbia)

1966
The Movie Song Album (Columbia)
A Time for Love (Columbia)
Singer Presents Tony Bennett (Columbia)
The Oscar (Columbia)

1967
Tony Makes It Happen! (Columbia)
For Once In My Life (Columbia)

1968
Yesterday I Heard The Rain (Columbia)
Snowfall: The Tony Bennett Christmas Album (Columbia)

1969
Just One of Those Things (Columbia)
I've Gotta Be Me (Columbia)

1970
Tony Sings the Great Hits of Today (Columbia)
Something (Columbia)

1971
Love Story (Columbia)
Get Happy (with the London Philharmonic
    Orchestra, Columbia)

1972
Summer Of '42 (Columbia)
With Love (Columbia)
The Good Things In Life (MGM)

1973
Rodgers & Hart Songbook (DRG)
Tony Bennett Sings: "Life Is Beautiful" (Improv)

1974
The Tony Bennett/Bill Evans Album (Fantasy)

1976
Together Again (Improv)

1977
*Tony Bennett, the Mcpartlands and Friends Make
    Magnificent Music* (Improv)

1984
Chicago (DCC)

1985
Anything Goes (Columbia)

1986
Art of Excellence (Columbia)

1987
Tony Bennett: Jazz (Columbia)
Bennett/Berlin (Columbia)

1990
Astoria: Portrait of the Artist (Columbia)

1991
40 Years: The Artistry of Tony Bennett (Columbia)

1992
Perfectly Frank (Columbia)

1993
Steppin` Out (Columbia)

1994
MTV Unplugged (Columbia)

1995
Here's to the Ladies (Columbia)

PHOTOGRAPHY CREDITS

AP/World Wide Photos: pp. 18,19 left

Archive Photos: pp. 14, 17, 33, 62

©William Claxton: pp. 41, 48–49

Dale Parent Collection/©Robert W. Parent: pp. 10, 16

Everett Collection: pp. 3 right, 52-53, 58, 69, 95, 107, 109

FPG International: p. 23

Frank Driggs Collection: pp.15, 20, 31, 32, 44

Globe Photos, Inc.: pp. 2 right, 19 right, 46, 55, 65, 70, 72; ©Ralph Dominguez: p. 78; ©B. Fitzgerald: p. 83; ©Richard Fitzgerald: pp. 51, 64; NBC: pp. 22, 39, 47; ©Bob V. Noble: p. 99; ©Lisa Rose: p. 102; ©Jay E. Silverman: pp. 60, 61, 66, 71; ©Hy Simon: p. 82

©Herman Leonard: pp. 2 center, 28–29, 36

LGI Photo Agency: ©Karen Pulfer Focht: p. 110

Michael Ochs Archive: pp. 34, 85 both

Personal Collection of Tony Bennett: pp. 2 left, 12, 13

Personality Photos, Inc.: p. 40

Photofest: pp. 24, 26, 30, 38, 50 both, 56, 86–87

Photoreporters, Inc.: ©James Colburn: p. 92;
©Phil Roach: pp. 77, 100 bottom

Popperfoto: pp. 3 bottom, 94

Ray Avery's Jazz Archives: pp. 4, 80

Retna, Ltd.: ©Larry Busacca: pp. 8–9, 88, 96–97; ©Steve Double: pp. 91, 98; ©Steve Eichner: pp. 100 top, 101; ©Gary Gershoff: pp. 3 top, 73; ©Steve Granitz: pp. 90, 105, 108; ©Sam Levi: p. 93; ©Joe Marzullo: p. 104; ©Frank Micelotta: p. 74; ©David Redfern: p. 67; ©Scott Weiner: p. 106; ©Richard Young: p. 76

Reuters-Bettmann/Blake Sell/Archive Photos: p. 103

Rex USA LTD.: ©Brian Rasic: p. 111

Star File: ©Bob Leafe: p. 79; ©Irv Steinberg: 54; Vinnie Zuffante: p. 81

©Chuck Stewart: pp. 37, 42–43